Dedication

To Kathy, my wife, for teaching me gentleness.
To Priscilla, my mother, for teaching me inner calm.

Acknowledgments

I feel a deep sense of gratitude toward the many people who assisted me in the writing and completion of this manuscript. My wife, Kathy, and my son, Paul, were invaluable in terms of their support, patience, and encouragement. Greta Coalson and Lynn Gonzales provided their enthusiasm and commitment to the arduous task of typing and retyping. I also owe a great deal to Margaret Kutcher for her devoted and painstaking work of editing. Working together we were all able to make the publication of this manuscript a reality, for the honor and glory of Him.

About the Author

Dr. Paul DeBlassie III is a clinical psychologist. He completed his doctoral training at Colorado State University and Northwestern University School of Medicine. Dr. DeBlassie is director of the Christian Psychological Center in Albuquerque, New Mexico, and is also the founder of the Christian Psychological Foundation, a non-profit organization that serves the Catholic and general Christian communities with seminars, workshops, and retreats that focus on depth psychology and family living.

Contents

Foreword

This book is a very valid effort to harmonize the ancient religious practices of meditation, together with the modern insights of the medical sciences, in an effort to discover the key to *inner calm*. Today it is being recognized that true medical practice must be concerned with holistic healing. It is no longer sufficient for medical practice to concentrate solely upon the physical or the psychological or the emotional, or even the spiritual. On the contrary, recognizing that each of these components of the human person are essentially interrelated, it becomes imperative to address that root cause of the lack of inner peace and calm that might, in turn, affect each of the other areas of the human person.

The thesis of this manuscript states that inner peace can be cultivated by the disciplined practice of the Jesus Prayer. The Jesus Prayer is an ancient Christian prayer in which the name ''Lord Jesus'' is meditatively focused upon for two 20-minute periods per day. Dr. DeBlassie uses this brief prayer as a source of his examination of the relationship between depth psychology and meditation. It is his thesis that the daily practice of this prayer precipitates positive psychological change and contributes to a strong and deepened spiritual life.

Living in an age that has seen incredible change in our social condition and living habits, there is little wonder that modern people are desperately struggling to regain inner calm and peace. Medical research has shown that Christian meditation, such as described in this book, increases personal emotional tranquillity and well-being. Harvard University has focused medical research on the positive physical benefits of daily meditation. It has been recognized that the Jesus Prayer, when practiced twice per day, has had a marked impact upon reducing cholesterol levels and high blood pressure, contributing to healthy functioning of the central nervous system as well as the muscular and cardiovascular systems.

It must also be mentioned that a healthy spirituality can only be the result of the integration of the psychological and the physical. Persons who have experienced psychological and physical benefits in their lives as a result of Christian meditation will naturally find themselves drawn more deeply into the practice of their own Christian and Catholic faith. In this book specific methodology for practicing the Jesus Prayer is suggested not only for adults but also for children and for families. Throughout the section on spirituality, references are made to the Fathers of the Desert, Saint Teresa of Avila, Saint John of the Cross, and other mystical Doctors of the Church.

And finally, we should recall the words of the psalmist, "Be still, and know that I am God. . . ." (Psalm 46:10) If, indeed, we are people of faith, we will heed the word of our God spoken to us through the psalmist. It calls us forth to an inner calm, to an environment where we can recognize the presence of God. It is precisely this union between the human and the divine which is achieved through the practice of the Jesus Prayer. I am pleased to recommend this book to every person who is serious about achieving an inner harmony with self and peace with his or her God.

Robert F. Sanchez
Archbishop of Santa Fe

Be still,
and know that
I am God....
Psalm 46:10

1
CHRISTIAN CALM

Stress and Calm: Jesus and the Christian Life

Jesus, from the intensity of the stress he was undergoing, prostrated his being before the Father, seeking the consolation that results from knowing the Father's willful caring. Saint Luke records his agony:

> *"Father, if thou art willing, remove this cup from me; nevertheless not my will, but thine, be done." And there appeared to him an angel from heaven, strengthening him. And being in an agony he prayed more earnestly; and his sweat became like great drops of blood falling down upon the ground.* (Luke 22:42-44)

In actuality, stress can reach such magnitude that the sympathetic nervous system responds by secreting a fluid from the sweat glands that appears to be blood. Being aware of this fact, we can better appreciate the great love that Jesus expressed for us throughout his life and especially during his agony and crucifixion. Human in all ways save sin, Jesus empathized with our human condition. Each of us has day-to-day experiences that test our capacity to endure wounds that can leave their mark on the soul. As Christians, we have the consolation of knowing that there was One who went before us, the Suffering Messiah. His physical body responded to stress just as ours does. And yet he announced that, in the end, the overcoming victory is ours.

Stress and Conflict with Others

Our day-to-day stresses reveal themselves in small ways. For example, after a particularly difficult day at the office, at home, or wherever work takes us, we may try to settle down, only to find ourselves restless and ill at ease. Rather than deal directly with the person we have disagreed with during the day, we bring the frustration home and displace it on wives, husbands, children, even the family dog. Unless we confront and work through the trying moments as they appear, accumulated tensions slip out and wound the ones we care most about.

Frank, a busy and successful business entrepreneur, came to me complaining of feelings of depression that seemed to have arisen spontaneously. As we began talking, it became clear that he was well respected by all of his colleagues and regarded as diplomatic in all of his business dealings. By and by I discovered Frank's secret. Outside the home he rarely opposed anyone. Instead, he would try to smooth things over and be as diplomatic as possible.

But at home with his wife and children he would complain about every least irritation, from the children speaking too loudly to the paper being read before he could get to it. His persistent bickering often caused fights and upset the entire family. In time, Frank became aware that he was the one responsible for the lack of harmony, a fact for which he berated himself and felt more and more guilty, to the point of becoming depressed.

Like all of us, Frank needed to learn that suppressing daily annoyances frustrated the love he so much wanted to share with his family. As he and I dealt with the importance of confronting his colleagues at the right times, we witnessed the surfacing of a deeply buried fear. Frank thought that if he would dare to be confrontive, his anger would become unmanageable, eventually hurt others, and cause them to disrespect and shun him.

As this fear was worked through in therapy, Frank found that he could confront his co-workers without exploding in rage, without harming relationships, and without losing the respect that was so important to him. In fact, some of Frank's closest friends at the office commented that he was much easier to work with because his opinions and true feelings were more accessible to them. As he became more accessible as a human being with deeply felt emotions, Frank gained more support and respect from his peers than ever before.

Needless to say, Frank's family life settled into more harmonious and understanding relationships. He no longer found himself quibbling about trifling matters. When conflicts arose in the family, he directly addressed them so that they would not blow up out of proportion. This experience led Frank to look even more deeply into his soul and to learn from his stress.

Jesus, Stress, and Inner Quiet

Frank's unheeded symptoms of stress had manifested themselves in interpersonal conflict. Stress can also make its effects felt through headaches, stomach problems, ulcers, and other more serious diseases. It has often been said that the epidemic of modern times is hypertension, a by-product of too much stress for too long a time. Hypertension can precipitate atherosclerosis, heart attacks, and strokes. It is estimated that hypertension alone takes its toll in fifteen to thirty-three percent of the American population annually. In fact, more than fifty percent of deaths in the United States each year can be attributed to diseases of the brain and heart.

Somehow, as I ponder these facts, I cannot help wondering if Jesus experienced some of the same physical afflictions that beset us today. Surely, during his brief life-span, the Master must have undergone more stress than any modern-day man or woman would dare to imagine. Could it have been that even he felt the ravages of stress to the point of being hypertensive?

Perhaps I am biased in my assessment of the character of Jesus. But it seems to me that he was such a man of peace that a deep serenity and harmony of spirit and body encompassed him, overriding any tendency toward physical ailments caused by stress. The great reservoir of peace in the person of Jesus really is not compatible with any debilitating accumulation of anxiety and stress. Physiologically, when an individual becomes anxious, adrenalin is secreted in abundance throughout the system, and the concentration of thyroxine increases. If we experience long periods of unrelieved anxiety, those substances tend to take their toll in serious physical symptoms. Therefore, in order to avoid inner tension and the consequent physical repercussions, Jesus must have had some way of releasing and detaching himself from everyday strains and burdens so as to experience inner calm and physical rest.

His great secret of being able to calm himself is apparent in the Scriptures. As he did during the agony in the garden, Jesus withdrew from his daily activities in order to seek the Father and his peace whenever confronted with a momentous task. We can imagine Jesus being sensitive to the still, quiet voice within him that echoed the words of the psalmist,

> *As a hart longs*
> *for flowing streams,*
> *so longs my soul*
>   *for thee, O God.*
> *My soul thirsts for God,*
>   *for the living God. . . .*
>   (Psalm 42:1-2)

In following this inward urge to seek the presence of the Father, Jesus found the serenity that nourished and filled him.

The tasks and decisions that confronted Jesus were of monumental bearing on the future of humankind. We all know how making decisions that affect others' lives taxes us emotionally and physically. At one time I worked in a crisis clinic, where I was responsible for determining whether or not the suffering souls who walked into the facility needed to be hospitalized. In turning away some and admitting others, I frequently felt the burden of having made a decision that would have significant, lifelong impact for many of them. How profoundly aware Jesus must have been that his daily decisions — where to preach, when to allow himself to pull away from the pressing needs of others in order to pray — would influence the course of salvation history!

As persons who exercise responsibilities that touch the lives of others, it is important for us to remember this fact: before beginning his formal ministry, Jesus followed the inner call to go to the desert for forty days and nights to be in communion with the Father (Luke 4:1-13). During that time in the desert, Jesus encountered the stillness that has been the training ground for holy people and prophets down through the ages.

I remember my first visit to Christ of the Desert Monastery, away in a canyon of fertile desert in the New Mexico mountains. When I arrived, the kindly Brother who met me told me that many people come there to find spiritual comfort in the silence. Instead of discovering contentment of soul, however, many of them are frightened by the contrast between their inner stress and the tranquillity of the desert, where God gently makes known the inner workings of the heart. This is the very way Jesus was prepared, the way he learned to quiet himself at times of stress during his ministry, so that he could hear the soothing voice of his Father.

Jesus and Quiet Prayer

There are other instances in which Jesus quieted himself. The Scriptures record that before he chose his disciples, *"he departed and went into a lonely place."* (Luke 4:42) We can imagine Jesus rising before anyone else in the morning and finding a solitary place in which to immerse himself in the Father. In the very early hours of the morning, I have found, my own spirit seems quite fresh in perceiving him who is the All in All. Especially in the desert, the setting where Jesus prayed in the early hours of the morning, all of creation seems to come together to worship the Father. At this time worldly happenings have not yet clouded our spiritual sensitivities. We have the luxury of taking him in purely as his being fills us and surrounds us. Truly, this is a spiritual happening with the Father, Son, and Holy Spirit. With what great clarity of mind and conviction of spirit Jesus must have approached the task of choosing his disciples after such an uplifting experience!

Perhaps it was Jesus' daily desire to seek the Father's touch in prayer that prompted one of the disciples to request, *"Lord, teach us* [emphasis added] *to pray."* (Luke 11:1) At the very least, the disciples must have noticed, with some curiosity, that their Master would rise before any of them and return looking fresh — as if he had been anointed — to begin the work of the day. Peter was probably stumbling around to start the fire, still groggy with sleep. He was probably startled to hear Jesus ask him if he needed help, because he hadn't noticed Jesus' absence. With what surprise and wonder Peter must have looked at the Lord! As incident after incident took place in which one or another of the disciples encountered the spiritual discipline of Jesus, the entire group finally decided to ask him to teach them to pray. They wanted to learn how to acquire this discipline that would allow them time before the start of a day to fill their hearts with the peace of Yahweh.

The wisdom of the Church has always emphasized the example of Jesus seeking restfulness of spirit received in prayer. Saint Augustine (A.D. 354-430) noted that this serene contemplation consists of focusing on the presence of the unchangeable God, "the Light Unchangeable." In his book *The Third Spiritual Alphabet,* Francisco de Osuna, a sixteenth-century Spanish Franciscan, advocated finding a quiet environment for retreat into prayer, as was the custom of Jesus. Osuna wrote:

> Although these practices and others like them may be very good, if you wish to advance further and imitate loftier things, our letter advises you to frequent recollection and become an expert in it, thus emulating Our Lord, who used to go out into the desert where, apart and recollected, he could more secretly and spiritually pray in concealment to his and our heavenly Father.

Saint Teresa of Avila, who was guided by Fray Francisco's writings on prayer, commented in *The Way of Perfection:*

May the Lord teach this recollection to those of you who do not know about it, for I confess that I never knew what it was to pray with satisfaction until the Lord taught me this method. . . . Anyone who walks by this path keeps his eyes closed almost as often as he prays. . . . It is a striving so as not to look at things here below.

We can discern similarly ardent instruction in learning the way of prayer from the sayings of the Fathers of the Desert:

Abbot Arsenius, when he was still in the King's palace, prayed to the Lord saying: "Lord, lead me to salvation." And a voice came to him saying: Arsenius, fly from men and you shall be saved. Again, embracing the monastic life, he prayed in the same words. And he heard a voice saying to him: Arsenius, fly, be silent, rest in prayer: these are the roots of non-sinning.

The inspired movements of Jesus toward prayer have stirred up inner longings for quiet contemplation in Christians throughout Church history. In the life of Jesus we are struck by the profound peace that he was able to maintain while undergoing fierce inner battles and stresses. Like the saints of old, we, too, are called by the Spirit to claim our inheritance of peace — a peace that quiets us in the midst of storms and surpasses all understanding (Philippians 4:7).

Stress and the Christian

Each of us is well acquainted with feelings of stress. In one way or another, our lives challenge us with situations that can seem overwhelming at times. Like David in the Psalms, we feel like coming before the Lord and crying forth, *"O LORD, my God, I call for help by day."* (Psalm 88:1)

I remember a client coming into my office and saying, "I'm so uptight that I feel like a bundle of nerves. Everything irritates and bothers me. I'm wondering if anything can help at this point,

Doctor DeBlassie.'' As he told me this, the man fidgeted and spoke very rapidly, hardly pausing to take a breath. He went on like this for at least twenty minutes, and during this time I sensed what his heart was desperately trying to communicate to me. Camouflaged by anxieties were yearnings that lie deep within each of us, yearnings for peace.

Before me I saw someone whom many would refer to as a dynamic and saintly man. He had been involved as a deacon in his local church for ten years. He was a respected leader and teacher. He had brought many to experience a revolution in their lives through following Jesus. He was regarded as an influential business executive in his hometown, and could buy anything the world had to offer. Yet, the longings of his spirit were profound. A divine call seemed to beckon him to go deeper into the kingdom of heaven within, to even turn aside, if need be, from the external activities that occupied so much of his time — to be still and experience God.

After the man had settled down enough to tell me more about the history of his problem, he gave me some very enlightening information. I learned that his psychological and medical histories involved symptoms of high blood pressure, episodic migraine headaches, periodic feelings of overstress, anxiety, and a recent upsurge in marital and family tensions and disputes. Things had slowly been worsening over the past five years.

The man had sought a number of different avenues for relief from these ailments of body and soul. His pastor offered him the rite of Reconciliation through confession. That had afforded him a brief respite from his inner struggles. But in his conscience he was not aware of any form of blatant sin or consequent guilt that might have precipitated his painful condition.

In his prayer community this client's fellow elders prayed and interceded for him. As hands were laid on his head, he felt the inner surety that the Good Shepherd was beside him. A close friend offered him a word of encouragement, saying that the present turmoil would lead him to heights of faith-experience, that only those who taste the fruit of suffering from the Mount of Olives (Matthew 26:42) grow to enjoy the inner peace and light that comes after the struggle (Romans 8:17).

The client's physician, a Christian man of mature years, diagnosed this situation as an inordinate amount of tension that had eventually erupted both physically and psychologically. For the physical symptoms, the physician prescribed a proper diet and medication for hypertension. For the psychological part, he referred the patient to our clinic, to be under the care of a Christian clinical psychologist.

Fortunately, this man heeded his physical symptoms; he recognized them as expressions of psychological and spiritual disharmony. Within six months his blood pressure was back to normal. His headaches subsided, and his family conflicts were beginning to be resolved. All of this began to happen as he realized that growth in peace was crucial for health as well as for spiritual progress. Inner peace is not a fringe benefit of the Christian life; it is a primary experience of a life surrendered to Jesus.

Surrendering to God

As the years pass and as I minister within Christian communities, I am in touch with more and more men and women who are experiencing unmet needs like those of this pastoral leader. A prominent church leader once remarked to me that, in seeking to minister within his church, he had become so busy and tense that his inner life of prayer, reading, and reflection had practically dried up. His ministry was causing tremendous inner pressure. He no longer sensed the infilling of God's power and was now having to rely on his own resources. He seemed to be taking one step forward and two backward in all that he did. On his knees one night in prayer he surrendered this need for feverish activity to the Holy Spirit.

Once he had surrendered, he realized that he had forsaken his inner life and chosen a way of driven involvement in order to enhance his own ego by proving that he could accomplish great things for God. Such egocentric activity had left him spiritually high and dry. After reorienting himself, he was able to allow the Father to mold and sculpture his life. This new direction brought about an inner movement from distress to peacefulness. What a remarkable difference he experienced in "letting go and letting God"!

Fortunately, this pastor responded to the quiet voice within him. Not everyone answers the inner call in such a positive manner. We tend to make up excuses for our eventual bad disposition that results from being so distressed. We are tempted to blame job problems, family members, friends, and even our childhood for inflicting discord upon us. It is as if we run faster and faster from the realization that we are responsible for our own predicament.

Naming the Demon: Prolonged Stress

With regard to life's problems, the Desert Fathers are frequently quoted as saying that once the demon has been named it ceases to exert its power. For this reason, it is essential that we become acutely aware of the inner demon, prolonged stress and anxiety. Long-term, unrelieved stress — with its eventual deadly product, physical and psychological distress — is the plague of many Christians who are overworked and underrested. The remedy lies in pulling out of the descending spiral of anxiety and distress by unconditional yielding to the quietness of God.

This yielding illustrates what Jesus meant when he said, *"Come to me, all who labor and are heavy laden, and I will give you rest. . . . For my yoke is easy, and my burden is light."* (Matthew 11:28,30) The word *rest,* as used in this passage, comes from the Greek word *anapausis,* a term used to describe how a farmer rests his land by sowing only light crops. How sensitive is the Lord! As we receptively embrace him, he removes the yoke that consumes our strength, allowing us to be rejuvenated.

Time and time again I have heard people complain of the massive loads of distress that burdened them before they found liberation in a life wholly resigned to Jesus. A woman approached me one night at a church where I was teaching. She confided in me about troubling family matters that threatened to overwhelm her. She was extremely frightened by external crises and internal depression. As we prayed together, she spontaneously relinquished her burden. She accepted the inner surety that God was at work and could do far more for her family than she could do by all of her worrying. The depression lifted, and her spirit seemed to soar with a newfound freedom. The woman discovered that liberation from inner distress emanates from surrender of the tense self to God.

Stress Causes Illness

It has long been recognized that tensions cause illness. Physicians are now saying that fifty to eighty percent of all diseases and illnesses can have stress-related origins. The story is told of a physician who was suffering from an irritating stomach ulcer. He knew just enough about psychology to think that he could trace the cause of the problem back to long-held resentment against his father. One day as he was sitting quietly in prayer about this, he thought: "Whether or not I have resented my father, even more critical is the fact that I have often resented my *heavenly* Father. I have resented his commandment to turn away from self-seeking, to go out of my way to love the most unlovable people in my life if I am to truly follow him." As he accepted this awareness, the ulcer cleared up. His experience demonstrates that tension can produce illness and psychological strain, but that it can also make us aware that something needs change and transformation.

Most clinical psychologists and physicians agree that the following illnesses can be classified as stress-related: hypertension, peptic ulcers, ulcerative colitis, mucous colitis, atopic dermatitis, Raynaud's syndrome, hay fever, arthritis, enuresis, migraine and tension headache, general sexual dysfunction, sleep onset insomnia, and a great majority of neurotic and psychotic disorders.

When it is mentioned that these disorders are stress-related, I find that people immediately say, "But they are real. It's not just in my head." That's right. It is important to understand that these illnesses are very real. The fact that they originate with feelings of extreme stress over a long period of time does not diminish their reality. Whether caused by family problems or some sort of personal strain, psychological stress always affects the body. It immediately causes the hypothalamic and reticular systems in the brain to send a message to the endocrine system that stress hormones need to be released. Eventually, the sympathetic nervous system is activated; peripheral blood vessels constrict and various muscles become tense. The hands may feel cold because blood that normally keeps them warm is moved to other parts of the body. The heart also may be affected; typically it races faster and faster. Such manifestations are very real, yet they can be induced by psychological stress.

Over a long period of unrelieved stress, the body tends to lose its natural capacity to relax and readjust itself to a restful state. A stockbroker who was referred to me for stress management had been in high stress for so long a time that his peripheral blood vessels had adjusted themselves to remaining constricted. This caused severe migraine headaches. Sometimes he would even wake up in the morning with a migraine.

Through stress-management training, the stockbroker learned to dilate his peripheral blood vessels and raise his hand temperature at will. Acquiring this skill helped him to achieve a refreshing state of relaxation in usually no more than a few minutes. The benefits were so great that eventually he incorporated this technique into his daily prayer time. He now looks forward to his prayer time in a way he never had before. In a deeply relaxed state he feels open to the presence of God in a new way. Thus, prayer time is of benefit physically as well as spiritually.

Making Use of Available Remedies

One of the most difficult tasks in life is to learn to grow psychologically from stress. In contemporary society we see an upsurge in the use of medication to treat psychological as well as physical problems. I am convinced that medication is a valuable therapeutic aid in treating certain severe disorders. However, when we are confronted with an inner storm, it is far too easy to rely on medication to soothe us rather than to look within ourselves. If we take the trouble to explore the thoughts and feelings associated with our anxiety, the resulting insight will lead to personal growth. The difficult part is that facing up to our problems may initially cause even more anxiety. Nonetheless, the searching is necessary if we wish to resolve and expel the source of anxiety once and for all.

The prophet Hosea declared rather forcefully, *"My people are destroyed for lack of knowledge."* (Hosea 4:6) I have found that Christians often fear that seeking help may imply to others that they have not been leading a God-filled life or that their ailment is a result of sinful living. Thus, they try to hide their inner tensions. Many Christians are caught in this predicament, yet their walk with Jesus is strong and pure. They surrender as much of themselves as they know today to as much of Jesus as they know today. It is painful to see them suffer for so long because of their unwillingness or inability to find a spiritually sensitive physician or psychologist.

The dilemma seems to smack of an insidious but blatant negativism that pervaded the Church in the past. For many years we have doomed ourselves to narrow-minded thinking that does little to proclaim the kingdom of God. Instances abound. When Sir Francis Drake discovered the potato in Peru and tried to introduce it into Scotland, the people rejected it because the potato is not mentioned in the Bible. In Boston, when street lamps were first being used ministers decried them, proclaiming that if God had intended things to be brighter he would have made the sun and the moon more brilliant. For years the use of any type of anesthetic for women giving birth was practically outlawed by the Church in France. It was thought that pain was the result of original sin and therefore not to be interfered with. Even today this hurtful, narrow-minded attitude sometimes prevails. It is time to recognize the full range of ministry that is available to the Body of Christ.

Admitting Our Need

The apostle James dealt profoundly with this issue when he wrote, *"Humble yourselves before the Lord and he will exalt you,"* and again, *"Is any among you sick? Let him call for the elders of the church, and let them pray over him."* (James 4:10 and 5:14) The message in these verses seems to be one of humble admission of our limitations and hurts. As members of the Church, each of us is called to meet the needs of our hurting brothers and sisters. In turn, our needs are also to be met by the Christian community.

Even for a Christian, the constriction caused by ego-centeredness and pride blocks inner transformation and feels quite burdensome. This is because pride harnesses the individual with a yoke of self-sufficiency. Secretly or openly, a person who is so burdened has this attitude: "I have the power to do all that I want to do; I don't need anyone or anything. I may pretend that I need others, but I really don't feel that I do." A total disintegration of such a rigid attitude is needed before the fullness of peace can be experienced. As we humbly admit our feelings of inadequacy and burden before the Lord and our fellow believers, the pinnacle of egocenteredness and pride disintegrates. This disintegration permits a tremendous sense of freedom to be released within.

The Church is not a museum of saints but a hospital for sinners. The very paradox of the Gospel message centers around the need to admit our sinfulness humbly in order to open our hearts to the glory that fills the saints of heaven. As we humble ourselves, so shall we be exalted. We are as saintly and strong as we are humble.

The Father constantly permits the course of life to humble us so that we may enter into a life of peace. As we grow closer to him, many hurts and pains of the past begin to surface. This happens in order that we may be humble in our need before him. We may have suppressed long-standing emotional hurt in order to avoid facing the more painful aspects of being human. But in the course of life the Father makes us aware of past stresses and the way they still influence us so that we can learn and grow from them. If we hide them away, we learn nothing. A client once told me, "As I admit my neediness and face what I have feared looking at for so long, I am able to experience release and relief."

Hidden Feelings and Attitudes

Stresses in the guise of past fears can be very deeply buried in the subconscious. In his Letter to the Romans, Saint Paul sensed the depth of the Holy Spirit's healing touch in the subconscious mind as he wrote, " . . . *be transformed by the renewal of your mind, that you may prove what is the will of God, what is good and acceptable and perfect.*" (Romans 12:2) As the subconscious mind is dealt with, as we become aware of hidden-away attitudes and feelings, it becomes possible for Life to exist within our very depths. It is as if our subconscious can either harbor old grudges and resentments or it can exude Life. If the grudges are removed and Light and Life penetrate our spirit, then the subconscious radiates a power that we can live by.

Depth psychologists have frequently noted that most of our mental activity transpires below the level of conscious awareness. We have all had this experience: we say or do something spontaneously, and then, afterward, we realize that it had great bearing on a situation that is currently preoccupying us. A rather dramatic example comes to mind. A friend once told me of her great concern over the fact that she felt no grief when one of her aunts died. For weeks after the funeral she went around humming a tune under her breath. She did this quite obliviously until someone asked her why she kept humming, and sometimes whistling, the same tune over and over. When she thought about it, she realized that she was humming the melody to a song with these words: "Ding, dong, the wicked old witch is dead!" Needless to say, she was taken aback at the implication of her behavior. Consciously, she in no way felt even the slightest irritation with her aunt. While the aunt was living, my friend had often made a special effort to drop in or send a small gift, especially during the holiday season. She had continued to do this even though the aunt never so much as said "Thank you." But below the level of her conscious awareness, my friend entertained a great deal of resentment toward the aunt, who had caused much anxiety in earlier years. Together my friend and I explored her old feelings and attitudes, and we discovered that she had made a conscious effort to block out her underlying bitterness and resentment toward the aunt. She had attempted to change her conscious thinking and behavior without paying heed to the vast depths of her subconscious feelings.

The stresses that we deposit in our unconscious seem to push forward constantly for conscious recognition and resolution. Jesus referred pointedly to the repressed or suppressed impurities that are within: *"Woe to you, scribes and Pharisees, hypocrites! for you cleanse the outside of the cup and of the plate, but inside they are full of extortion and rapacity. You blind Pharisee! first cleanse the inside of the cup and of the plate, that the outside also may be clean.''* (Matthew 23:25-26)

If that is not strong enough for us, Jesus further declares: *''Woe to you, scribes and Pharisees, hypocrites! for you are like white-washed tombs, which outwardly appear beautiful, but within they are full of dead men's bones and all uncleanness. So you also outwardly appear righteous to men, but within you are full of hypocrisy and iniquity.''* (Matthew 23:27-28) Thus the Scriptures exhort us to bring to light, to awareness, the hidden inner strifes that ravage us.

Becoming Aware of Unconscious Conflicts

The message of the New Testament Letter to the Hebrews is critical to inner re-formation:

> *For the word of God is living and active, sharper than any two-edged sword, piercing to the division of soul and spirit, of joints and marrow, and discerning the thoughts and intentions of the heart.* (Hebrews 4:12)

In this passage we can find scriptural support for the surfacing of unconscious conflicts and tensions. When we try to discern the thoughts and intentions of the heart, we discover that they are not always immediately accessible or understandable to us. It is therefore critical that we become aware of the unconscious conflicts that perpetuate distress in our lives. Confronting our inner self generates a sense of release and freedom. As Jesus so poignantly stated, *'' . . . you will know the truth, and the truth will make you free.''* (John 8:32)

By helping us to focus on thoughts and intentions of the heart that cause distress to accumulate, the Word of God leads us to a release from inner tension. In place of inner tension, we find peace through self-knowledge gained from insight and inspiration inherent in the Word. Thomas à Kempis makes this point in *The Imitation of Christ:*

He to whom the everlasting Word, that is, Jesus, speaks, is freed of many vain opinions. From that Word all things proceed and all things openly show and cry that He is God. Without Him, no man understands the truth, or judges rightly. But a person to whom all things are one, and he who draws all things into one and desires nothing but one, may quickly be made firm in heart and fully at peace in God.

Dwelling within us in his divine nature, Jesus beckons Christians to surrender all that is in the conscious mind and all that is in the unconscious. Once we do so, we can hear the Holy Spirit speak the words, "Peace! Be still!" A young woman I was working with came to see me one day after a distressing confrontation with her mother. The problem was that the older woman had been indulging her grandchildren in an excessive way. Whenever she heard that their mother had refused the children something, the grandmother would rush out to the store and buy whatever it was that the children wanted. Then she would present the gifts to the children, saying, "That mother of yours tries her best, but she just doesn't know how to love you like your grandma does. Grandma will always take care of you." All of this greatly disturbed the children's mother. But the younger woman wanted to avoid any direct confrontation that would cause the grandmother to feel rejected by a seemingly ungrateful daughter. These thoughts provoked so much conflict within my client that she couldn't sleep at night. She lost the inner peace she had enjoyed up to this point.

As we worked through some of the conflict together, we began to see that whenever she was threatened with rejection by her mother, she would frantically look for ways to make reparation. This time, however, she realized that her relationship with her children was at stake. Her conflict centered around the need to express her concern to her mother. But she knew that if she expressed that concern, she would be risking rejection. At the end of our session, the origin of her distress had been clarified: on the one hand there was her desire for approval from her mother; on the other hand was her desire to assert her deeply held convictions. Struggling for clarity in the matter, she became aware of a need to spend time alone to ponder the implication of this insight.

As she sat in her room praying, reading, and thinking, she came across these lines in Scripture, *"I will never fail you nor forsake you. . . . I have called you by name, you are mine."* Reading these lines filled her with an inner surety that she was always loved, no matter what, and that she would always be taken care of. In her words, "It's as if the presence of God took over, to love me and care for me when my mother's love seemed to stop. God's love now fills the empty spots that I had desperately wanted my mother to fill."

The next day she sat down with her mother and explained to her how difficult it was to be confrontive in this matter. She even told her how she feared rejection. This was perhaps the first time that the young woman had been so bold with her mother. Much to her surprise, her mother just sat and listened quietly. Then, surprisingly, the mother apologized for her indiscretion. She began to share her awareness that maybe she wanted to give too much to her grandchildren; maybe she had been trying to make up for the ways she had neglected her own daughter. Talking about their feelings left the mother and daughter much better able to express their care and concern for each other without fear of rejection.

Inner Quiet Brings Personal Wholeness

The Word of God freed this young woman so that she could deal with her inner stress in a direct, honest, life-changing way. The Scriptures brought out her hidden thoughts and feelings so that she could be aware of them. When this kind of awareness soaks into our psychological self, it is as if an intense light shines within us. As the psalmist says,

> *Thy word is a lamp to my feet*
> *and a light to my path.*
> (Psalm 119:105)

Like this young woman, many of us search so frantically for peace that we muffle the ever-present inner voice, "Peace! Be still!'' Saint Teresa of Avila describes the experience of ceasing this restless striving, entering into inner quiet:

> This quietude and recollection is something that is clearly felt through the satisfaction and peace bestowed on the soul, along with great contentment and calm and a very gentle delight in the faculties. It seems to the soul, since it hasn't gone further, that there's nothing left to desire and that it should willingly say with Saint Peter that it will make its dwelling there.

In describing this experience, the repose of the faculties, Saint Teresa is talking about the sense of physical and mental rest that accompanies inner quietness. The inner self releases tensions and anxieties, and dwells in a state of oneness within. The body and the mind also respond by entering into a deep repose and rest. I have heard many individuals say that this experience rests their body and mind far more than many hours of sleep. Inner harmony seems to rejuvenate our physical faculties as well as our mental ones.

For too long many of us have approached the problems in an either/or way. We view them either as psychological/spiritual or as physical in origin. What these approaches fail to recognize is that physical and psychological aspects intertwine and affect each other. Fortunately, many individuals are beginning to regard their physical and psychological symptoms as possible expressions of personal psychological and spiritual disharmony. Among the churches, some denominations are becoming open to a more balanced perspective in their ministry.

Modern scientific discoveries are revealing the mutual effect of the inner self and the physical self. In John 5:14, Jesus tells a paralyzed man to go his way and sin no more. What Jesus is implying here is that a person's inner state affects the person's body. Both the Gospel and modern science express this conformity between body and psyche, a reality that we are often aware of in simple ways. For instance, on days when we feel distressed or troubled, we can easily notice a lack of physical energy. Conversely, on days that are harmonious and peaceful, we experience enthusiasm and a sense of physical well-being.

Appreciation of this vital connection can help us to be convinced that growth in peace is crucial for physical and psychological health, as well as for steady spiritual progress. The way we feel does not depend totally on nerves and muscles. Solid and deep inner peace contributes greatly to our physical and psychological well-being.

The psalmist's utterance, *"Be still, and know that I am God,"* urges us gently but definitely to seek peace — the peace that sustains and gives life to the human spirit. This is the peace that transforms distress into harmony and wholeness within our spiritual and psychological foundations.

2
THE PSYCHOLOGICAL FOUNDATIONS OF STRESS

Freud's Beginnings

Dynamic psychologists agree without a doubt that Sigmund Freud (1856-1939) pioneered the exploration of anxiety as a debilitating factor in human life. Others, such as Kierkegaard and Nietzsche, focused on anxiety as a critical determinant of human behavior. But only Freud analyzed anxiety with the conviction that it formed the basis of various psychological disorders.

Freud postulated three forms of anxiety: realistic, neurotic, and moral. *Realistic* anxiety refers to anxiety resulting from perceived danger in the environment. That is, the individual experiences an objective threat to his or her safety. The term indicates the presence of a real situation that would be described by most people as anxiety-provoking.

Freud asserted that realistic anxiety was precipitated by the first major trauma of life — the birth trauma. He conjectured that this initial trauma laid the groundwork for a reaction of anxiety to other traumatic environmental situations. The birth trauma threatens the experience of life as the infant knows it within the womb.

There are conflicting opinions regarding the beginnings of consciousness in human life. But whether or not we believe that infants experience birth anxiety, it is obvious that babies gasp, cry, and kick during the birth process. For our purposes we will define this as anxiety.

Realistic Anxiety in the Gospels

The Scriptures abound with descriptions of such realistic anxiety. Consider, for instance, the Lord and the disciples at the Mount of Olives. Prior to leaving for the Mount, the Lord had already been comforting his followers with words such as, *"Let not your hearts be troubled; believe in God, believe also in me."* (John 14:1) With much intensity he went on to tell them that he would send the Holy Spirit to comfort and guide them. Did the disciples really grasp what Jesus was speaking about at this time? I find no indication that they did. All they knew as they approached the Mount was that the Master had been speaking of his death and trying to console them.

We can imagine the growing sense of uncertainty and stress in the disciples as Jesus took Peter, John, and James to a secluded spot to pray. Surely the three must have heard Jesus as he cried, *"Father, if thou art willing, remove this cup from me; nevertheless not my will, but thine, be done."* (Luke 22:42) The disciples may even have seen the drops of blood he was shedding. We can imagine Peter returning to the others and saying, "He is in so much pain! Surely something terrible is about to happen!"

It is recorded that Jesus spent additional time in prayer. When he rose, he found his beloved disciples sleeping. We may be inclined to reproach the disciples for falling asleep at such a stress-ridden moment when the Lord needed them most. However, if we take a look at our own lives, we can discover why they were sleeping. When intense stress and anxiety are present, our physiology sustains a terrible blow. One way to recuperate and regain a sense of energy is to retreat into sleep. This happens quite naturally. When we are most stressed and anxious we also feel drained and depleted of energy, especially if the anxiety continues for a prolonged time. The disciples may have tried their best to remain awake, but their bodies were urging them toward sleep in order to dissipate some of their anxiety and renew a sense of energy.

The anxiety resulted from seeing their Master in such agony. But it also came from the fear of losing him in death. He had provided a new life for them — a life that met their inner needs for spiritual and emotional nourishment and their outer needs for daily sustenance. Much as a child perceives safety, comfort, and caring from his mother as she holds him in her arms, so the disciples knew the solace of the constant presence of Jesus. This is why they dreaded the separation he frequently spoke of.

The separation anxiety that tormented the disciples vividly portrays the realistic anxiety of which Freud spoke. The apostles had left their trades and, in many cases, even their families to follow Jesus. They had trusted themselves to him without reserve. Now their very lives seemed to be in danger. In their minds, all that they had sacrificed and worked for would come to nought with the death of Jesus. A sense of danger and fear of the unknown, without Jesus, gripped their souls.

At this time Jesus had not yet sent the Comforter. The Comforter, psychologically, would fill the disciples with the presence of Jesus so that they would know he was always within them. A small child practices independence and permits separation from its mother only when it senses enough of the mother's love to feel secure in that love, even when physically separated from her. If a child does not incorporate the mother's loving presence adequately, due to some fault in the mother-child relationship, then the child will become anxious and upset whenever the mother's physical presence is not apparent. It is normal for a very young child to be upset and anxious in this way. With constant and consistent caring, however, the child eventually does feel secure in the mother's love.

In the same way, before they were spiritually mature, the disciples panicked as they anticipated the physical absence of Jesus. But with the coming of the Comforter, the very essence of Jesus filled the disciples to such a degree that this realistic separation anxiety went away.

The Case of Sally

A young woman — I will call her Sally — came into my office complaining of panic attacks whenever she would leave her home without her husband at her side. These attacks had been happening for years and had been a source of much discomfort to her. Finally, her family doctor advised her to seek professional help. She heard of me through her pastor and decided to see me.

As Sally told me about her feelings of panic and the extreme hardship it had caused her and her family, she seemed to be highly motivated to explore feelings, thoughts, and memories. As we progressed in psychotherapy, she recounted childhood feelings of abandonment by her mother. During preschool years she had been left alone at home while her mother went out to work. At first the isolation troubled her, but eventually she adjusted to being alone. She developed imaginary friends and playmates. The problem was that she adjusted to such a degree that she became very anxious whenever her mother prodded her to leave the house and play with other children. It should be mentioned that her mother and father had divorced when she was only two years old.

During the course of therapy, Sally recalled weekend visits from her father. He would take her to the park and spend an entire afternoon with her. Only during those times did she feel safe enough to leave her home. Unfortunately, her father always left after just one day. And, when he would leave, so would her sense of safety and protection out in the world.

When she reached school age, Sally was forced to go out into the world despite her terror. The first few days of any school year were particularly difficult. But Sally learned to cope with her anxiety by becoming the teacher's pet. Being cared for in that special way helped her to cope. At the end of high school, Sally met a man who, much like her father, gave her a sense of comfort and security. Once they were married, she anticipated that all problems would be taken care of. For all practical purposes they were, except when she needed to leave home without her husband and confront the world on her own.

By this time, Sally's fear had become partially a realistic fear; because of her shelteredness, she had not learned how to get along in the world. She had not learned how to shop for herself, how to find her way around a new town, or even how to meet new people. If she had been left to her own resources, she would have had much to be concerned about.

With the support of her loving husband, we were slowly able to work through this gripping anxiety. As she was freed from it, Sally also experienced the fatherhood of God in a newer, deeper way. In her words, "He is so totally within me that I now feel that there is nothing to fear."

Neurotic Anxiety

The second type of anxiety, which Freud called *neurotic* anxiety, arises out of what psychoanalytic psychology terms "ego-id relations." That is, an individual essentially perceives his or her instinctual demands to be quite dangerous and fearsome because of the external danger associated with fulfilling these instinctual demands. Rollo May, in his book *The Meaning of Anxiety,* summarizes Freud's theory by saying that

> . . . the individual experiences libidinal impulses which he interprets as dangerous, the libidinal impulses are repressed, they become automatically converted into anxiety, and they find their expression as free-floating anxiety or as symptoms which are anxiety equivalents.

Unlike realistic anxiety, a response to external danger, neurotic anxiety represents the repression of various instinctual drives or needs. In neurotic anxiety the individual treats intense instinctual demands from within as equally dangerous as threats from without. In Freudian terms, the ego fears the demands of the id.

Within church circles this Freudian position has often been misunderstood. I have heard many pastors condemn Freud for advocating what they termed "a permissive morality." Without a doubt, Freud was reacting to the Victorian prudishness of his times. It is not hard to believe that pent-up sexuality and nurturance needs made many a person of the Victorian era quite neurotic. However, we must keep in mind that Freud was referring to the extreme repression of sexuality in his era, repression that left many individuals badly scarred. Essentially, he was saying that repressed sexual and nurturance needs will eventually create psychopathology.

Perhaps this point can be made more clear with an example. Julie, a woman of twenty, came to see me one day because of feelings of depression. For reasons unknown to her, these feelings left her with a constant sense of emptiness and apathy. Julie had been living with this intense pain for at least three years.

As we explored her history prior to the state of depression, we found that Julie had lost three significant people in her life. The first was her fiancé. In the process of planning to marry, she had learned that the man was seeing her best girl friend on the side. A big argument had ensued, and ended with her losing both the fiancé and the girl friend. Then, six months later, her favorite aunt died. This aunt had provided her with much of the nurturance and love that her mother had failed to give. The aunt's death was followed, ten months later, by the unexpected death of Julie's oldest sister. By this time, Julie was in a state of depression, feeling that those she was closest to had suddenly been torn away from her.

In therapy, we began to see that along with these feelings of loss was a feeling of anger. Julie felt that those she trusted most had either betrayed or abandoned her. She knew that the feelings toward her aunt and sister were unreasonable, that their deaths could not be helped. Yet the feelings persisted. For three years she had tried to pretend that the feelings were not real. She did all that she could to talk herself out of them, to run from them. However, in her own words, she found that "the faster I run away from them the stronger they seem to get."

Julie had decided that she would never again allow herself to experience closeness with another human being. She walled herself away from intimacy and closeness. With candidness she admitted, "It's safer in here; I won't get hurt. I don't even have to let you in, Doctor DeBlassie."

As the weeks passed, it became more and more evident that Julie desperately wanted closeness and the nurturance that comes from relationships. In Freud's terms, her instinctual desire for intimacy and closeness had been repressed to the point of causing depression. On the one hand, she yearned for closeness and for a trusting relationship. On the other hand, she was afraid to let herself be vulnerable and open to hurt.

Slowly, as Julie began to allow herself to feel the fright of being hurt, a new openness developed between us. As she became aware of her feelings and began to understand them, the fright suddenly became less threatening. In the process she felt herself trusting me and allowing a closeness to develop between us. Over the course of many months, she progressively opened up not only to me but to others as well. She began forming new relationships and experiencing, once again, the ability to trust. Incidental to this, her depression lifted. It seemed that once she responded to her natural needs to be involved in caring relationships, she no longer felt depressed. As the fear of closeness was worked through, she was able to respond to and fulfill her needs for closeness. Consequently, she no longer felt crippled by depression — or, as Freud termed it, by neurotic anxiety.

Moral Anxiety

Freud referred to the final type of anxiety as *moral* anxiety. He felt that anxiety of this sort typically manifests itself as guilt feelings in the ego and consequent feelings of fear in one's conscience. The conscience, representing internalized parental authority, threatens to punish the individual for any transgression of the perfectionistic goals of the superego implanted by the parents.

Experience tells us that moral anxiety need not be confined to parental upbringing. Other authority figures such as teachers, aunts and uncles, and even the Church easily impress small children as being very powerful and influential. One's sense of morality and conscience is generated from past experience with influential figures delimiting right and wrong.

In Old Testament times, it was the Torah that prescribed morality. Jewish children were raised to adhere rigidly to the Law set forth in the Torah. A person living in that day did well to conform to it, for strict punishments were levied against transgressors. Take, for example, the severe and harsh rulings against disobedient children:

> *If a man has a stubborn and rebellious son, who will not obey the voice of his father or the voice of his mother, and, though they chastise him, will not give heed to them, then his father and his mother shall take hold of him and bring him out to the elders of his city at the gate of the place where he lives, and they shall say to the elders of his city, "This our son is stubborn and rebellious, he will not obey our voice; he is a glutton and a drunkard." Then all the men of the city shall stone him to death with stones; so you shall purge the evil from your midst; and all Israel shall hear, and fear.* (Deuteronomy 21:18-21)

Israel's most powerful king, David, felt the pangs of moral anxiety. In chapter 12 of the Second Book of Samuel, David apparently was gloating over the prosperity of his kingdom and his recent victories. This gloating contributed to a sense of spiritual idleness that caused him to be led astray by sin. From atop his palace one day, David noticed a very beautiful woman named Bathsheba. Without considering the fact that she was another man's wife, he fell in love with the woman. David had already married several times in defiance of the Law, which stated that a man should only have one wife. When he saw Bathsheba, he decided to take her, also, as his wife. After this, it seems that his sense of anxiety led him to commit one sin after another.

Instead of confessing and doing away with his pangs of guilt, he chose to try and cover up his sin. He ordered Uriah, Bathsheba's husband, home from the army on furlough. His plan was for Uriah to have sexual relations with Bathsheba so that her pregnancy would appear to be proper. However, Uriah did not manage to engage in the relaxed conduct that would have permitted David's plan to succeed. So David then decided to place Uriah in a dangerous position on the battlefield, where he would certainly be killed. Once Uriah was killed in battle, as planned, David married

Bathsheba. She was already pregnant with his child. Throughout this time David secretly harbored his sin and spent long hours in heartache and pangs of conscience. David described his anguish of soul thus:

> When I declared not my sin, my body wasted away
>   through my groaning all day long.
> For day and night thy hand was heavy upon me;
>   my strength was dried up as by the heat of summer.
>   (Psalm 32:3-4)

After the birth of the child, the Lord provided an occasion for David to acknowledge his sin and seek forgiveness. The Lord sent the prophet Nathan to tell King David a fictitious story with the intent of opening up his conscience. Nathan related:

> There were two men in a certain city, the one rich and the other poor. The rich man had very many flocks and herds; but the poor man had nothing but one little ewe lamb, which he had bought. And he brought it up, and it grew up with him and with his children; it used to eat of his morsel, and drink from his cup, and lie in his bosom, and it was like a daughter to him. Now there came a traveler to the rich man, and he was unwilling to take one of his own flock or herd to prepare for the wayfarer who had come to him, but he took the poor man's lamb, and prepared it for the man who had come to him. (2 Samuel 12:1-4)

David was enraged by the cruelty of the rich man in the story, and he declared:

> As the LORD lives, the man who has done this deserves to die; and he shall restore the lamb fourfold, because he did this thing, and because he had no pity. (2 Samuel 12:5-6)

Nathan looked at David and said, "You are the man." Then he went on to enumerate David's wrongs and the blessings God had given him. David bowed his head in sorrow and confessed his wrongdoing. After seeking the Lord in humbleness of spirit and with a contrite heart, David was able to write:

> *I acknowledged my sin to thee,*
> *   and I did not hide my iniquity;*
> *I said, "I will confess my*
> *   transgressions to the LORD";*
> *   then thou didst forgive the guilt of my sin.*
> *Be glad in the LORD, and rejoice, O righteous,*
> *   and shout for joy, all you upright in heart!*
>   (Psalm 32:5,11)

A Case of Moral Anxiety

The suffering of moral anxiety is what led David to repentance. In many ways, moral anxiety is a God-given feeling meant to lead us away from immorality and toward honesty and truthfulness of heart. The Scriptures teach that moral anxiety is not meant to cause permanent pain but, rather, to incite a repentance that will bring relief and freedom to the spirit.

A middle-aged man who was considering psychotherapy shared with me his feelings of anxiety and guilt. For many years he had been drinking himself into a stupor every weekend. In his drunken state he often engaged in homosexual activities. Eventually, his sense of conscience motivated him to seek help for the feelings of torment that plagued him.

He clearly described his predicament: "I think that I drink in order to stop the screaming of guilt within me. When I wake up in the morning after one of my episodes, it's as if I just don't want to even look at myself in the mirror. For a long time I thought I could run from the guilt and not have to look at what was causing me to act in ways that left me so empty. I have a sense that this whole thing of psychotherapy isn't going to be easy. Looking inside yourself and coming to grips with the truth never is. But the faster I run, the larger the problem becomes. It is just getting to be too much for me."

As we began psychotherapy, he became aware of many areas of his life that had been hidden away too long. He recalled times when, as a child, he saw his father severely beat his mother. If he called out in protest, the father would turn on him verbally and physically, saying, "You're good for nothing. You'll never be a real man. See how afraid of me you are."

Seeing his mother hurt so terribly and being quite unable to help her reinforced his feelings of inadequacy and fear. The inability to help the person he loved most meant that, surely, nothing of any substance existed in him. Added to that was a crippling fear of his powerful father that immobilized him.

As a man, he noticed that whenever he dealt with a powerful authority figure, especially a male, he would cringe. His boss frequently took advantage of this obvious fear by requiring him to do extra work with no pay, under the threat of losing his job. He suppressed his anger at the demeaning attitudes and behavior of others.

His feeling of inadequacy and self-diminution grew. Over and over, he backed away from interpersonal confrontation until he was withdrawing in isolation from almost any kind of social gathering. More and more, the only way he could subdue his feelings of anxiety and worthlessness was by drinking.

Drinking gave him a temporary exuberance and confidence that set him more at ease socially. In fact, he often livened up family events and parties with his wit and humor. However, his problem increased as he gradually required more and more alcohol to produce the necessary exuberance and confidence. The more he drank, the more obvious his flight from life became.

Along with fleeing from life's responsibilities, he felt terrorized by interpersonal relationships. Men made him feel lowly and powerless. Women caused him to feel guilty and inadequate because he did not project certitude and confidence. Increasingly, he recognized that he felt strong only with timid, dependent males.

His upbringing had taught him Christian values that he felt were quite at odds with his life-style. The drinking, now almost uncontrollable, still enlivened him socially. The homosexual relationships briefly gave him the nurturance and caring he yearned for but felt incapable of obtaining in an acceptable way. But with each periodic drinking or homosexual episode, anxiety escalated until it overwhelmed him.

In the succeeding months of therapy, he came to perceive that anxiety and guilt actually motivated him to seek inward wholeness and integration as he probably never would have otherwise. The surfacing of past hurts and resentments opened him up to the experience of forgiveness and caring, both within the therapeutic relationship and within his newfound relationship with God. He discovered that in running frantically from his fears he actually had been turning away from the wholeness and psychological integration that desired to become manifest within him.

To deny and run from anxieties and fears leaves only the option of constantly fighting the ghosts that pursue us. Once the anxiety or fear surfaces and comes into awareness, the ghosts vanish. As the letter to the Ephesians so poignantly states, *"When anything is exposed by the light it becomes visible, for anything that becomes visible is light."* (Ephesians 5:13)

The Heart of the Self

After Freud, psychodynamic psychology expanded in a number of directions. One very influential school of thought viewed personality development as the result of past interpersonal relationships: an individual's psychological state reflects accumulation of interpersonal experiences that have either strengthened or weakened the person's sense of self-worth.

Harry Guntrip, the author of *Personality Structure and Human Interaction,* has been a primary exponent of this concept. Guntrip refers to the heart of the self as a force constantly striving for integration and wholeness. The growth of the self is nourished by experiences of acceptance, caring, and love.

The main deterrents to developing inner wholeness and self-worth are fear and anxiety. Fear here means the sharp, intense feeling that results from encountering an intimidating or hurtful person, especially during childhood. Such an experience causes withdrawal in order to protect the self from hurt and psychological injury. This fear can frequently be observed in a child being disciplined. Typically, the child withdraws from the situation not only by stopping the behavior but also emotionally. This fear is healthy in the sense that it helps to form the child's conscience and ability to act in socially appropriate ways. Ideally, after the child encounters disapproval over behavior, the parent needs to communicate the caring that motivated the reproof so that the child maintains a sense of inherent goodness and worth.

Spiritual Discipline

In one of the church congregations that my family and I belonged to, there was a father who personified loving discipline with his children. One look from him would usually settle down an unruly youngster. If a scolding was needed, the father would talk sensitively with the child. The father conveyed both the firmness required to deal with rambunctiousness and the caring needed to assure the child of his father's constant love.

These words of Scripture come to mind: "*. . . he disciplines us for our good, that we may share his holiness.*" (Hebrews 12:10) God's caring touches us through the discipline of the spiritual life. The discipline need not be long-lasting; its purpose lies in drawing us closer to God in order that we may partake of his holiness.

A friend of mine stated it clearly: "All the difficulties that we encounter in life are purposeful. Troubles and difficulties can teach us much about the need for honesty and balance in our lives, if we pay heed to them. If we dismiss them as irrelevant occurrences, then it seems that they need to return until we learn what the Father wishes to teach us. I remember how, for a time, I was constantly involved in frustrating situations that made me furious and angry. One after the other, I dismissed these situations as coincidental. Finally, I took time to realize that I had been missing what life was trying to teach me for my own growth, to see that these situations glaringly brought out my selfish need to have things my own way without regard for anyone or anything. Once I came to this awareness, whenever frustrating situations came my way, I consciously recognized that I needed to have things my own way in order to prove how strong and controlling I was, as if to cover up a very real but underlying feeling of inadequacy.

"As I looked, I gradually began to see that I need not become rageful in order to prove myself and my self-worth. My self-worth is something that is so much a part of me and so deeply ingrained naturally that I can afford to let situations be as they will be and not feel that I always have to conquer them. I'm a man of fifty, and you would think that I should have realized this far earlier in life; but I guess I'm hardheaded enough that it took a few times before I was able to profit from what life brought my way. It's strange, but somehow I don't really feel bad about having been so angry for so long in these frustrating situations. I just needed them so that I could learn. As I look back I feel that God was very patient and sensitive with me in never permitting a sense of guilt or self-condemnation. He knows how much I need to learn and how much I need his love all along the way.''

The False-Self

Unfortunately, rather than learning from an anxiety-producing situation and thereby releasing the anxiety, many persons feel themselves subject to a persistent and prolonged state of fear. The experience of continuous fear in interpersonal situations has been termed anxiety. Guntrip and other authors like him see anxiety as a conveyor of the prolonged and debilitating quality of the fear. For our purposes, the distinction between anxiety and fear need not be a major concern. Suffice it to say that the temporary, fleeting experience of fear does not have the negative and debilitating characteristics of the prolonged experience. The continuous psychological perception of fear eventually exerts crippling effects.

Incessant fear progressively perpetuates a feeling of psychological splintering and breakdown. I do not mean to imply that the individual in any way manifests outward behavioral signs of the inner disintegration. In fact, a person who harbors a great deal of inner fear may compensate for this by appearing extremely outgoing and friendly in social situations. However, this gregariousness usually projects an underlying quality of superficiality, which Guntrip refers to as the false-self. At the depths of the false-self manifestation resides a very wounded and splintered heart. The false-self, in essence, assists the individual to function on a day-to-day basis. It is as if the false-self aids in providing a semblance of cohesion for the splintered, wounded, hidden-away personality.

The more I come in contact with people who manifest such a false-self, the more I realize the profundity of Jesus' exhortation, *"Judge not, that you be not judged."* (Matthew 7:1) Time and time again I see men and women who had intensely fear-ridden childhoods. They were not given adequate psychological nourishment, nor did they develop the strength to cope with anxiety-ridden parents. Distorted ego-growth always has its basis in such fear-ridden early relationships. This fact can help us to understand the teaching of Jesus to love and be compassionate rather than to judge; we never know the pain or inner agony that prompts unloving behavior, thoughts, and feelings.

A Case of False-Self

An instance of the prominence of the false-self occurred within a church meeting I was involved in. One of the participants was haranguing those in charge. Her complaints centered on what she considered to be a lack of spiritual depth in the teachings. The leaders tried to be as responsive to her as possible, but nothing they did seemed to satisfy her.

The disgruntled woman soon developed a following. There were people who looked up to her because she was very convincing in her arguments. They felt inspired by her conviction. So a group within a group developed. The splinter group found its purpose largely in faulting the administration and leadership.

As the conflict persisted, the church leaders decided that perhaps the best remedy would be to invite this woman to speak before the whole group — eight hundred people or so — and to deliver teachings that she considered to be of suitable spiritual depth. When told of the decision, the woman accepted the invitation. At the same time — but only for a brief moment — she seemed frightened.

On the night of the scheduled talk the crowd waited to hear what this outspoken woman would have to say. As time passed, she failed to arrive. Everyone, including members of her own group, wondered where she was. It seemed unthinkable that she would not take advantage of this moment that she had fought so long for. After an hour of waiting, the leaders decided that something must have come up.

The leaders had no idea how close to the truth they were. A great deal had come up — from within the woman herself. After the meeting a member of her group, a close friend, went to her house to make sure everything was all right. When the friend knocked at the door, no one answered. She noticed that the door was unlocked, so she let herself in. As she entered, she heard quiet sobbing from the bedroom. Even when the friend walked into the bedroom, the crying woman did not notice her presence until the friend reached out to embrace her. Then they began to talk, and the friend learned what had happened.

A few hours before the meeting, all the fear that had been hidden within the woman came to the surface. Fear gripped her and immobilized her. The more she fought against it, the stronger it became until she broke down in tears.

As the friend held her, the woman still felt the pangs of the fear. Fortunately, the sensitivity of her friend helped her to realize that the fear resulted from not paying heed to a process that was going on within her. As the two women explored that fear together, the message behind the emotion became clearer.

Later on, the woman began to express the depths of her fear by writing out her feelings and sharing the images and thoughts that came to mind. As she did this, she became increasingly aware of the meaning of her fear. She discovered that she had been pretending for so long to be so strong and invulnerable that she had forgotten what prompted her to act as she did in the first place.

From childhood she had experienced so much inadequacy, loneliness, and fear of people that she had decided to overcome all of this by acting in a way that was contrary to her feelings. She had done this for so long that she saw it as role-playing. She actually considered herself confident and socially at ease. Throughout the years she had never had to prove herself in any way that would strain this acquired sense of confidence and poise — until the conflict with the church group cracked the facade. Beneath her false-self dwelt a trembling heart. In fact, the woman's entire body shook as the fear revealed itself.

Expressing this fear to her caring, accepting friend allowed her to go on and explore its meaning. Slowly, the fear seemed to pass as she talked about the other feelings associated with it. She and her friend decided to meet on a regular basis to continue the process of exploration. Their meetings continued for several months. During that time many hidden memories and feelings surfaced. Together, the two women worked through many suppressed and repressed emotions.

For a long time fear had been trying to gain awareness in the woman's consciousness so that she could integrate its meaning — that she yearned for acceptance and closeness with others. The thought of possible rejection and hurt had prevented her from establishing such closeness. When fear threatened to incapacitate her, she decided to manifest the false-self of tenacity and boldness. This facade allowed her to hide the terror in her heart.

As a result of her healing experience, this woman saw that exposing even her rawest feelings did not lessen her friend's genuine caring and love. Their bond of friendship gave her a hope that others might also accept and respect her for what she was, with no pretense of strength. As she risked being herself with others, she experienced a new freedom. She accepted her limitations and strengths, and she also received affirmation from others.

Her times of prayer and meditation took on a new character. Relaxation and quietness entered into her prayer times. In her words, "He just seems to hold me as his child." Previously, she had thought that she needed to generate a multitude of pious words and acts of contrition before God would touch her with his presence. Now prayer became a time of serenity and quietness before God. Accordingly, she experienced even more inner integration and wholeness, which she expressed in this way: "I felt the meaning of the Scripture which says that he carved me in the palm of his hand and I am his."

This case demonstrates how all of our thoughts and feelings have meaning in relationship to the self within, to our brothers and sisters, and to Jesus, our Brother. Thoughts and feelings are on our side, so to speak. Yet, many people try either to cover them up or to cast them out rather than pay heed to them and integrate their meaning into the inner self. The message of Scripture definitely confirms that all of our inner thoughts, attitudes, and feelings always work together to bring us to more and more wholeness, more and more of an experience of Christ Jesus within:

> *We know that the whole creation has been groaning in travail together until now; and not only the creation, but we our-selves, who have the first fruits of the Spirit, groan inwardly as we wait for adoption as sons. . . . We know that in everything God works for good with those who love him, who are called according to his purpose. For those whom he foreknew he also predestined to be conformed to the image of his Son, in order that he might be the first-born among many brethren. And those whom he predestined he also called; and those whom he called he also justified; and those whom he justified he also glorified.* (Romans 8:22-23,28-30)

The Natural Self, Love, and Rebirth

In all cases, prolonged fear precipitates conflict between the conscious ego and the natural self that wills to live. Typically, the ego portrays a false-self while the natural self hides behind the conflict to avoid further pain. But at the same time, the natural self also desires to be released, to be reborn.

On a psychological level, these words of Jesus take on deeper meaning: *"Truly, truly, I say to you, unless one is born anew, he cannot see the kingdom of God."* (John 3:3) From a psychological perspective, this implies that one type of birth has already taken place within each person. The birth of the natural self coincides with physical birth. However, due to bad and painful experiences that tear at the worth of the natural self at a young age, this self withdraws into hiding. Such a psychological retreat serves to defend the self against further attack and bruising. Only when the Comforter comes spiritually and interpersonally will the natural self be reborn.

I emphasize the interpersonal element because many Christians think of rebirth as so "spiritual" that the effect of loving relation-ships can seem like a side issue. The fact is that fear can still grip the soul even after it has experienced spiritual reawakening. This fact may be unpopular among Christians who prefer to believe that spiritual reawakening suddenly makes the personality totally like Christ. This overspiritual attitude perpetuates a misunderstanding, if not a total lack of understanding, of the Gospel message to love one another.

In the Gospels Jesus constantly exhorts believers to nourish one another with love. He goes so far as to say that love may be so intense that one may lay down his life for the sake of a brother or sister. Even for the lowliest of the low, the least of his brethren, Jesus implores love.

To the Pharisee within us Jesus declares, " . . . *you tithe mint and rue and every herb, and neglect justice and the love of God; these you ought to have done, without neglecting the others."* (Luke 11:42) In the Church, how much more important it is to love the lonely one, the one without friends, the one no one pays attention to, than to busy ourselves with setting up committees, planning religious education programs, or organizing potluck dinners. All of these things are important, yes — but not to the neglect of self-sacrificing love.

Jesus goes on to say, " . . . *You shall love your neighbor as yourself."* (Matthew 19:19) As love touches the human heart the natural self begins to emerge. For this reason, actively manifesting love for one another nourishes and encourages the process of rebirth.

Loving the fear- and anxiety-ridden individual can be quite a challenging task. At times one may question whether such an individual has a capacity to respond to love. The crucial attitude involves always remembering that the natural self within each person retains the ability to love.

Results of the Lack of Love

The difficulties we have in loving persons who are fearful and anxious stem from the fact that their capacity to love has been frozen by early experiences of extreme hurt and rejection. Their early childhood relationships were meant to foster love. Instead, they broke into relationships of anxiety, fear, and interpersonal pain. Guntrip comments on this: "The living heart of him has fled from the scene, has regressed deep within, and he has lost his true self without which he cannot form loving ties."

Frustrated and unsatisfied love eventually overshadows the capacity to love. Continuing, Guntrip gives an example of how one of his patients described the experience of slowly losing the capacity to love:

> I was back in my childhood home with my parents, brothers and sisters. I had a lovely cake which I wanted to give them all, but they wouldn't have it and were not interested. I felt, "They don't want what I have to give." Then my eldest sister was making cakes and she wouldn't give me one of hers. I felt despairing. There was nothing to live for, and I went to my bedroom alone to lie down and die. My mother came in and said, "Don't be silly." She didn't understand at all.

Psychological damage of this sort motivates the damaged one to escape from the torturous dilemma. Resolution exists only in retreating from love, thereby closing off the possibility of being hurt.

In some cases the will to live and love has been so impeded that thoughts and feelings of death preoccupy consciousness. Usually, these thoughts and feelings consciously express the unconscious sense of psychic death. The heart of the self seems to have died as the result of the unsatisfied hunger for love. In such cases, suicide may be the outcome.

Unconsciously, the need for escape from the pain of frustrated love may lead to alcohol or drug abuse. Symbolically, drugs and alcohol signify the ingesting of a soothing object. Relationships only frustrate the longing for love and for the accompanying sense of soothing and calm. So, objects that do not involve relationships, that do not involve accentuating the inward hurt, are sought after to provide the nurturance so badly needed. Individuals who regularly intoxicate themselves claim that alcohol helps them to feel at ease about themselves, without a care in the world. They find a retreat from the world of unendurable frustration.

When relationships nourish the capacity to love, people feel good about themselves. Love causes the integration of a sense of self-soothing and peace. Infants nursing at their mother's breast quickly become quiet as they are fed, not only by the mother's milk but also by her loving gaze and the act of holding. As this quality of being cared for develops in relationships, children incorporate a sense of calm like that found with the mother. In essence, the capacity to love and feel soothed begins in the mother-child relationship, extends to the relationship with the father, and later involves the rest of the family and friends as well.

A Case of Fear and Rejection

I have used rather dramatic examples of fear in anxiety-ridden persons. However, people suffering intensely from fear and anxiety may not give even fleeting hints of their psychological condition. Also, the effects of fear need not be overwhelming or intense in our own lives in order for us to identify and empathize with the dynamics involved.

Susan, a well-known and respected woman in our church, confided in me that she had had a run-in with the pastor. More than any other person I knew in this church, Susan exemplified a depth of sensitivity and understanding of human predicaments. She could always be counted on to give others the benefit of the doubt. If she had been in conflict with the pastor, the situation must have been a serious one.

The particulars of the situation need not be recounted here. The crux of it was that Susan strongly believed in adhering to a biblical focus in the religious education program rather than a focus on matters of dogma. The pastor violently disagreed with her reasoning. He went so far as to tell Susan that he alone decided what would be taught; that if she did not agree, she could leave.

Susan felt enraged and inwardly torn by the conflict. The pastor had totally disregarded her fifteen years of service to the church. He had viciously attacked her and left her feeling bruised and wounded. Day after day Susan harbored feelings of anger and hurt.

These feelings gradually developed into the catastrophic fear that she had been rejected by the entire congregation. As the rejection and hurt intensified, Susan noticed herself not even wanting to see anyone from the church. Then, slowly, she began to realize that the sense of rejection and hurt had been magnified beyond proportion. Fortunately, her psychological sensitivity helped her to understand her need for intervention in this matter.

When Susan came to see me, three weeks had passed since her conflict with the pastor. In the course of trying to sort out her fear and anxiety, Susan had had a dream. The dream involved Susan kneeling in worship before a pompous, dark-clothed figure who towered above her. At the beginning of the session to which she brought this dream, she informed me that, after much thought, she understood the meaning of the dream. "Even my dreams show how subservient the pastor has made me. The dark-clothed, pompous figure represented the pastor. That's exactly what he wants me to do — kneel before him." As she told me of her interpretation, I thought how subtly the ego continues to defend against the conscious discernment of unconscious imbalance and conflict. As she and I explored her association with the dark figure, all of those associations indicated features of boastful pride, ego-centeredness, and self-seeking ambition. She agreed that the figure appeared to be the epitome of self-exaltation. I will never forget the expression on her face when I turned to her and said, "The dark figure in your dream is you." At first she laughed at my interpretation, failing to recognize any resemblance between herself and this haughty character. But she left my office that day feeling quite upset by the harsh implications of the dream.

The following night she had another dream in which she saw the proud and smug figure. This time the towering dictator slowly began to cringe, tremble, look panic-stricken, and then wither up and disappear. Susan's associations with this figure now centered on fearfulness and terror. She even went so far as to say, "He sort of dramatized how I've been feeling lately — full of fear and as if I'm withering up inside."

As we dealt with her feeling of withering up because of the fear, she started to comprehend how this cringing fear subsided for her only when she felt superior to those in authority. Up until now she had secretly prided herself in being far more sensitive and understanding of parishioners — and of people in general — than any trained professional or pastor could be. Now her insight poignantly asserted that behind that facade of sensitivity and humility there resided powerful forces of egotism and self-exaltation. Along with the self-exaltation could be found a fear that caused her to cringe in expectation of rejection.

During our sessions, we saw that she had used pride and egotism as defenses to prevent me from seeing and experiencing the fear within her. Humbly and sensitively she had begun the process of self-exploration with me. But as we encountered the pride within her, she used that pride to exalt herself over me and to reject my interpretations. As we dealt with her need to feel superior to me, she gradually permitted me to see her fear of being rejected, of being considered unspiritual.

In brief, Susan realized that even her seeming humility and sensitivity had been a pretense, a false-self. She had been hiding this false-self in a very proud and superficially exalted manner. Still, behind the pretense there resided the fear of rejection. The humility, her spiritual demeanor, even the pride acted to defend against the conscious realization of the fear.

With the help of these insights, worked through in our relationship, Susan found a new freedom in her life. Through this experience, a process of rebirth that had begun many years before with her conversion continued, dynamically and deeply. Susan's natural self emerged in a new way, without any dependence on false, contrived humility or secretly held pride.

Her new freedom so strongly inspired Susan that she visited her pastor to apologize for her stubbornness and insolence. Much to her surprise the pastor, also, apologized. He confessed that he had been so upset by the incident that he could only sit quietly before the Lord in prayer, waiting for some enlightenment. He admitted that to a great extent he agreed with Susan. But he felt that she was demanding her way without regard for other opinions. This feeling reinforced an old tendency he had of becoming stubborn and opinionated. He confided to Susan that he was becoming more and more aware of his inclination to close up and become rigidly defensive whenever his opinions were challenged.

As these two Christians opened up in love and sincerity, they witnessed the process of rebirth in each other. In true humility Susan shed her false-self and took the first step in reconciliation. Also in true humility, the pastor acknowledged the lack of charity in his own heart.

The experience of charity and warmth within relationships permits the emergence of the true heart of the self. Defenses piled upon defenses hide the fear and anxiety that cause the true heart of the self to feel lost within. The defenses may be typical ones involving denial and rejection, or they may consist of other emotions such as anger and guilt. Within the context of an accepting and caring relationship, a person can feel free to express these conflictual feelings and peel away the defenses one by one. Fear hides at the core of the false-self. As one passes through fear, the natural heart of the self emerges and radiates a sense of wholeness, humility, and calm, much like that of a child being held in its mother's arms.

Holding and Soothing

Oh LORD, my heart is not lifted up,
my eyes are not raised too high;
I do not occupy myself with things
too great and too marvelous for me.
But I have calmed and quieted my soul,
like a child quieted at its mother's breast;
like a child that is quieted is my soul.
O Israel, hope in the LORD
from this time forth and for evermore.
(Psalm 131)

This Scripture speaks of the serenity and quiet inherent in the natural heart of the self. Just reading it is soothing. The Word of God embraces and calms the weary soul.

The spiritual teacher Meister Eckhart (1260-c.1329) explains this peaceful union:

Neither is there anything in God that need be feared. All that is in God is only to be loved. And so there is nothing in Him that need make us sad. Who knows only His will and His wish, he is at peace. And no one is at peace save he whose will is utterly one with God's will. May God grant us this union! Amen.

Saint Teresa of Avila, in *The Interior Castle,* describes God's peace in this way:

Every way in which the Lord helps the soul here, and all He teaches it, takes place with such quiet and so noiselessly that, seemingly to me, the work resembles the building of Solomon's temple where no sound was heard. So in this temple of God, in this His dwelling place, He alone and the soul rejoice together in the deepest silence.

Saint Teresa focuses on the state of love-filled oblivion that encompasses the soul. Both she and Meister Eckhart agree that peacefulness and quietude of soul abound in the soul that loves God. These two Christian mystics emphasize the soothing and inner quietude experienced through union with God.

The inherent serenity within the self may also be fostered by human relationships that symbolically sustain the experience of being accepted, understood, and held. Psychological holding contains all of the qualities experienced in being held by God, except that on the interpersonal level acceptance, understanding, and caring are experienced explicitly. In the long run the experiences of being held and quieted by another person or being held and quieted in prayer differ little. He who is the All and All fills us with himself in the context of relationships of harmony and unity.

A very good friend of mine who is also a psychologist described the feeling of God's presence in caring relationships. He said: "When my patients and I meet for therapy, many psychological and spiritual happenings take place. On one level the contents of the unconscious surface to consciousness and make the patient aware of many hidden-away attitudes and feelings. On a deeper level these attitudes and feelings occur with the transference; they need to be worked through and resolved. The deepest level can hardly be described. As the unconscious rises to consciousness and the transference is caringly and sensitively worked through, a transcendency enfolds the patient and me. It is as if the very presence of God is with us and the very room in which we speak is hallowed.''

A former professor of mine, who specialized in treating severely disturbed patients, commented that in the depths of therapy patients often would come into his office, sit down, and comfortably relax and enjoy the presence of a caring person. Not a word would be spoken during these times. He likened this occurrence to a child being quite content in the presence of its mother. The sharing presence soothes, settles, and heals.

Testing the Relationship

This holding phenomenon transpires only after much testing of the relationship. A caring and warm relationship will always be tested for reliability. For many people, the risk of entering totally into a caring relationship revives memories of having been promised love time and time again, only to be let down and disappointed.

Because of such testing, the one who initiates the caring to the anxious person may feel quite taxed at times. It may seem that no matter what is said or done, the individual will not settle down into a trusting relationship. In fact, rather than reciprocate love and caring, the fear-ridden person may manifest only anger.

Typically, the anger emerges from accumulated and harbored resentments. Perhaps, for the first time, the suffering man or woman feels that at last a solid relationship can contain and eventually resolve the years of pent-up rage. The person frequently goes so far as to become hurtful and abusive so as to try to make the caring one actually feel the anger.

A patient of mine unconsciously enacted with me her experience of being left behind and considered insignificant. For quite a while we had seemed to be at an impasse in treatment. Then, quite spontaneously, she began to "accidentally" forget sessions. Each time this happened, I would lose an hour in waiting for her during the time we had scheduled.

In therapy we explored the issue of her lateness. At first she wanted to assure me that all of the misses had been accidental. After each missed session she would describe a convincing set of circumstances that had prevented her from keeping her appointment. In one case public transportation had been held up for thirty minutes, making it impossible for her to be on time. Another instance involved her forgetting about the appointment because of being off work on a legal holiday; she assumed that the clinic was also closed on the holiday. Throughout our initial exploration of the matter, she readily detailed circumstances such as these and denied any explanation except coincidence for these events.

At the end of the session, she looked at me and said, "I guess you know what I feel like in being left behind by everyone." Later sessions proved the unconscious motivation she had for making me feel the way she felt. She so much wanted empathy and understanding that she put me through actual circumstances to cause me to feel as she felt. With this insight and understanding, progress continued.

In the resolution of this patient's problem, a major portion of the dynamic depended upon containment of her feelings within our relationship. In the past, whenever she had attempted to convey her sense of loneliness, others had called her self-centered and weak. In no previous relationship had her feelings been contained and experienced by another.

Psychological holding can take place only when a person feels that the most intense and awful feelings can be accepted and thus contained by a caring other. Anger, fury, rage, and guilt all serve as defenses to ward off the fear of rejection and humiliation. But when a relationship has survived the storms a sense of safety embraces both persons. The safety implies the fortification of the relationship against emotional storms. Safety in a relationship kindles an awareness of being psychologically held by the caring other as closely and sensitively as a mother holds her child.

Psychological Safety in Infants

In a masterful book entitled *Maturational Processes in the Facilitating Environment,* David Winnicot describes the concept of holding in the mother-child relationship as ''not only the actual physical holding of the infant, but also the total environmental provision prior to the concept of living with. . . . It includes . . . experiences that are determined by the awareness and empathy of the mother.'' During this stage the mother and infant are as one. No psychological separation exists in the very early relationship of mother and infant. Neither mother nor child exists psychologically as a separate person. Only the mother-child relationship exists.

At times the mother seems to forget her own needs in order to attend to the needs of the infant. Mothers do without sleep for long periods in order to meet the plentiful needs of the infant. When the infant is distressed, so is the mother. When the mother is distressed or irritable, the child feels it and begins to cry. In all ways the mother and infant form a psychological union.

In healthy psychological development the infant learns to settle or soothe himself as the mother calms herself, thereby calming the infant. Slowly the infant begins to take on distinct psychological characteristics separate from the mother. This typically occurs when the infant feels safe enough to be curious and to explore the environment by means of locomotion such as crawling. At this early stage, if the infant encounters frustration or hurt, the mother's soothing is sought immediately.

Gradually, the infant ventures out farther and farther from the mother's presence. Feeling safe, due to the holding relationship with the mother, the child seems to carry that safety with him. The mother has fostered safety by psychological and physical holding, and now the infant projects that feeling of safety into the world.

Psychologically unhealthy development creates the opposite of these perceptions. The infant never feels safe enough to leave the mother. He continually returns to the mother in hopes of establishing an inner sense of being safely held. In such circumstances any separation from the mother fills the infant with anxiety.

In its extremes, an infant's lack of the sense of safety and caring precipitates severe psychological disorders in later life. The grown individual continues to regard the world as intensely hurtful, even annihilating. In an effort to cope with this hurt, the individual retreats deep inside, to the point of being out of touch with reality. Such regression literally manifests the person's need to return to the warmth and safety of the mother's womb. Not uncommonly, patients experiencing this need are found curled up in a fetal position in some corner. The need in humans for a sense of having been safely held, physically and psychologically, is indeed great.

Jesus and Psychological Holding

I am reminded of the incident of Jesus with the little children in chapter 18 of Luke's Gospel. We can imagine Jesus' weariness after preaching to the crowds all day long in the region between Samaria and Galilee. As he sat in the midst of the people, a sense of compassion and love must have enveloped them. Feeling the warmth of his words and the gentleness of his spirit, people waited for him to lay his hands on their children and bless them.

The charisma of faith and warmth must have indeed been great for those parents to have entrusted their children to the caring embrace and touch of Jesus. How many of us, after only hearing someone speak, would ask that person to touch and to hold our children? Through the Spirit within, Jesus touched the depths of the parents' hearts to such a degree that they did trust him to hold their children, perhaps in a way that they themselves had never been able to do.

We can imagine that, in one brief moment of being held by Jesus, each child achieved a satisfying inner sense of safety and caring. That moment of physical and psychological holding made up for any possible emptiness the child might have known as an infant. The loving clasp of Jesus satisfied the innate yearning to be totally embraced with care and love.

The implications of such a symbolic act in the ministry of the healing of memories are important. In this ministry, introduction of the symbolic image of Jesus is essential. The perception of an embracing Christ in the imagination produces a sense of caring and love that the person has never felt, or could even imagine feeling, from his or her parents. By returning to the early point of infancy, through memories, and allowing the image of an embracing Jesus to fill the person with a sense of being accepted, understood, and held safely, one intensifies the process of emotional healing.

Of course, the person cannot actually recall being an infant. Nonetheless, the psychological impression of the quality of infanthood remains. Hurtful impressions from infancy and childhood can only be re-formed by the symbolic impression of a new loving and caring person. One actually incorporates into the self the symbolic image and experience of being safely held and loved. In essence, the image of the holding Jesus heals and reforms the psychological impressions of infancy.

Interpersonal Holding

Experiencing the image of the holding and caring person also occurs on the interpersonal level. A client of mine commented on this experience: ''When I went home for vacation, I felt a moment of dread at the thought of having to approach my parents. I remembered their pressuring and belittling me as a child. Almost as soon as this happened, an image arose of you and me in therapy. The image caused me to feel at ease and at rest. Whenever I thought of you, I realized that I now deeply feel my own self-worth. Much of this feeling came from knowing how safe I felt with you in therapy and how much our relationship showed me that I am a lovable and loving person. When I actually saw my parents, I did not feel intimidated at all. In fact, my sense of ease helped me to see that even my relationship with them can be different. They no longer put me down as they did when I was growing up, so why should I continue to expect them to?'' At the conclusion of therapy, she told me: ''I'll miss you alright. But, you know, in another way I feel as if you're always with me, sort of inside of me. It's a good feeling.''

The symbolic taking in of the holding relationship prepares the person to function independently and strongly. Perceptions and attitudes change. As with this young woman, the ability develops for viewing life more objectively rather than from the perspective of past hurts. This independence replenishes the innate ability to enter into loving relationships without the impingements of past hurts.

The Process of Inner Integration

Internal re-formation should be regarded as a process. That is, one experience in the healing of memories or one therapy session usually does not affect dramatic change. As in the case of an infant, the person may at first seem passive about the healing experience. When an infant is first held and fed, he does not show any sign that he has gained strength from the nourishment; he may just turn and go back to sleep. But that is part of the strengthening process. It promotes an assimilation of the nutrients. The body is growing and developing toward independence.

Persons who have experienced authentic inner healing may want to be alone for a while. There may be no overt sign of healing and inner change. When this is the case, it is wise for the helping person not to press for information about the quality of the experience or feelings of change. At this point the psychological and spiritual nourishment needs to be assimilated into the inner self with the aid of quietness and rest.

People who are midway in therapy tell me that the experience is similar to taking in food. In this case, it is psychological food. A session's worth can give them a week's supply, so to speak. For this reason even one hour of self-understanding and further integration, out of the entire week, initiates and continues the process of growth and change. A little bit can go a long way in the realm of the psyche.

David Winnicott says that as the process of inner integration continues, the quality of passive dependence changes into a type of relative dependence. The *first* phase, absolute dependence, consists of passively being supplied with psychological food. The *second* phase, relative dependence, shows the person's *active* dependence on the healing relationship with the minister.

During the second phase, it is not unusual for people to call the minister or psychologist frequently, in order to obtain a sense that someone cares for and understands them even when they are not physically present. A little child accomplishes this by taking a few steps away from the mother and then looking back for a reassuring gaze. Gradually, the child can crawl or walk into another room, stay for an hour or more, and still retain the sense of the mother's concern and care. In the case of adults, their continued progress in inner integration brings them to the point where they realize their need for the one involved with them, then they actively seek to meet this need.

Persons in this second phase can function without making contact with the significant other person involved with them. However, they definitely feel more anxious and ill at ease until they can confirm the fact that someone else is aware of their situation and their inner storm. This awareness brings with it the security of knowing they have another person to depend on if the raging storm becomes too intense. That experience — that there is someone there who cares — helps them to face and work through their severest encounters with fears that formerly were deeply hidden.

Henry, a middle-aged man, had been involved in psychotherapy with me for a year. In the course of the year we encountered one storm after the other without any seeming breakthrough. He would call me once, if not twice, each week for assurance of my understanding and care.

Finally, one session revealed the ultimate fear that if he burdened others too much with his problems, the fury of his inner storm would destroy the relationship. As it turned out, the calls during the week often were meant to check in on me. In Henry's mind, the intensity of his emotions could have overwhelmed me. His greatest fear was that if he really allowed another person to know him, that person would be crushed by the wrath within him.

As Henry experienced the constancy of caring and compassion in our relationship, he faced his fears and furies one by one. He told me, ''As I see my fear for what it actually is, somehow it loses its grip on me. I don't feel enslaved by it. I have seen that you are not overwhelmed or crushed by my anger or fears. All of this relieves me of the burden of feeling that I was so bad that no one could take me if they really knew me. Now that all of this is out in the open, it seems like smoke that was thick and intense for a while but is now thinning out, sort of evaporating.''

The Final Phase of Integration

The third and last phase in the process of integration consists of a definite move toward independence. During this phase the infant's psychological development becomes sufficient so that constant maternal care is no longer required. The infant takes active steps toward existing and functioning without the constant watching or aid of the mother.

The infant reaches this phase through having accumulated memories of being cared for and nourished. The infant has become confident not only of mother's love but also of the love of the environment. Whenever this confidence is shaken, memories of being cherished and cared for come to the child's mind. This is not to say that the infant actually takes time out and deliberately remembers a time of maternal security and attention. Rather, a brief psychological impression, formed by accumulated memories of nurturance, serves to reorient the infant toward the inner sense that all is well within and without.

The course of this psychological development entails bringing into oneself the presence of the caring person. Infants psychologically incorporate the presence of all those individuals who have provided significant life experiences. Unfortunately, this involves both good and bad experiences with significant other people. To the extent that infants incorporate the presence of demeaning and fear-ridden people, they will think of themselves and the world as demeaned or demeaning and full of fear. The degree to which they incorporate the presence of nurturing, edifying, and confident people is the degree to which they will consider themselves and the world to be safe, secure, and loving.

In a clinic where I once worked, I recall walking in and seeing a very decrepit-looking, middle-aged man. I was told that this man had been coming to the clinic for years but had never wanted to become involved in therapy. He just sort of ''hung around.'' In this clinic, ''hanging around'' contributed to the overall milieu style of treatment. That is, part of the treatment consisted of permitting the patients to sit around the clinic, listen to music, talk with others, become involved in bingo, and participate in any other activity that was offered. This style was intended to foster a generalized sense of trust, a feeling that the clinic was available and supportive throughout the day. For several years this man had used the facility in that way.

The staff agreed that the man apparently had not yet developed enough trust in the clinic to be able to tolerate the more intimate, exacting atmosphere of individual psychotherapy. During my first few weeks there, I often engaged in casual conversation with him. We would talk, over a cup of coffee, about his extensive intellectual accomplishments. At other times, when I needed to walk across the street to another part of the hospital, he would ask if he could accompany me. During those short walks he would inform me about the latest happenings in sports, world news, even various occurrences in clinic community meetings I might have missed. He seemed to feel at ease with me, at least enough to confide in me about seemingly minor events.

Eventually, he asked to be considered for individual psychotherapy with me. I did have an opening at the time, so I accepted him for treatment. For this man, risking the challenge of entering pyschotherapy required several years of testing the trustworthiness of those at the clinic before he could — in his own words — ''take the plunge into treatment.''

A primary conflictual core for this patient consisted of feeling unattended to, uncared for, and consistently rejected. In fact, he had expected me to consider him unworthy to begin treatment. As he told me of his fears of rejection, I realized why he had delayed treatment for so long. Throughout the years he had had a strong desire to enter into treatment, but he always felt that the effort would end in failure, confirming his badness as a person. He needed and desired to trust in someone who would share his heart's sorrows and hurts, but he feared chastisement and rebuke for his wickedness.

One of the memories that surfaced for him in treatment revealed that, up to the age of eleven, he had sometimes soiled his pants. Each incident would set off great commotion in the family. His mother would be particularly perturbed. He recalled: ''Only at these times did she really know how much of a child I was. Sure, she would yell at me and tell me how terrible I was, but at least she attended to me, even if it was in a sort of negative manner.''

Family circumstances were such that the mother was involved almost totally with the care of her bedridden husband; she usually left her young son to fend for himself. He cooked his own meals, bought his own food, and took care of his life in general with little help from mother or father. Quite literally, the mother and father formed a unit that excluded him.

When the boy was twelve he was sent off to boarding school. There he progressed outstandingly in his academic work. At school he never had a problem with bed-wetting or soiling. But when he returned home for the first time, other symptoms appeared. His legs developed pains very similar to an arthritic condition. To alleviate the discomfort, the mother began rubbing his legs nightly with a special ointment that had been recommended by a physician. The efficacy of the ointment was doubtful, but one thing was certain — his mother attended to him and cared for him in a way that felt soothing and comforting.

Along with memories of his mother's soothing care, other memories surfaced — of her belittling him for needing so much of her time, time that should have been spent in taking care of his father. Occasionally, her anger would reach such intensity that she would refer to the child in the foulest of ways.

As treatment progressed, I began to be aware of signs that this patient was going through different developmental periods. During the first part of treatment, the patient felt very much dependent on me. At times he expected me to know how he felt without his telling me. His attitude closely resembled that of an infant, whose basic needs are taken care of by the mother without the infant feeling any sense of responsibility.

Outside of our sessions he would often linger around the clinic, looking very contented and relaxed. When I commented on his apparent ease he responded, ''You know, when I'm here I feel as if our sessions are going on, sort of like I'm with you. It feels good, sort of a warm feeling.'' By this time in treatment, he had already been internalizing the warmth and caring that he felt in our relationship. Even when he was not physically with me, he experienced the comfort of a caring presence. He no longer expected me to know his thoughts and feelings without having him tell me. He knew that our relationship was stable enough to contain the most severe of his feelings without endangering our bond of closeness. Even more important, the man was becoming more and more willing to risk speaking about the comfort and solace he found in realizing that I did not castigate or reprove him. In particular, he had anticipated incurring not only my reproof but also my wrath if he dared to let me know how much my attention and concern meant to him. At this point in treatment, the catastrophic expectation of belittlement associated with his need for trust and closeness began to be worked out little by little.

The effect of early relationships upon later emotional development can be readily seen in the sharing of this man. He had constantly prepared himself to receive the same wrath from others as he had from his mother. Lagging emotional development may result from any consistently injurious relationship. In this case the injurious relationship involved the patient's mother. In other cases fathers, aunts, friends of the family, anyone who consistently interacts with the child affects emotional growth and development.

During the first few months of a child's life it is the mother who provides the primary care. It is hoped that she also conveys the primary attitude of psychological holding. After these first few months, however, other family members contribute to a child's development of feeling held in caring relationships. The father can convey this feeling by his gentleness and concern in meeting the needs of the child, as well as by his firmness in discipline. Brothers and sisters provide psychological holding through their acceptance of the child in play and through watchfulness. Of course, brothers and sisters are not always quite so loving with one another. The important concern is that, in the long-range experience of the child, he or she is made to feel loved and cared for on a fairly consistent basis. Without a doubt, the more quantitative and qualitative love the child consistently experiences, beginning with the mother, the more deeply rooted is the experience of psychological holding and calm.

Holding and the Collective Unconscious

In his book *Psychology and Religion,* Carl Jung (1875-1961) comments on the soul's confrontation with anxiety:

There is a secret fear of the unknown "perils of the soul." Of course one is reluctant to admit such a ridiculous fear. But one should realize that this fear is by no means unjustifiable; on the contrary it is only too well founded.

In spite of the fact that Jung never really systematized a theoretical position regarding anxiety, he admitted — unfortunately, without much elaboration — that anxiety results from the fear of the dominance of the collective unconscious. In Jungian terms, the residue of subrational, archaic human functions extant within the personality may impinge upon the conscious mind to such a degree that anxiety threatens the personality. Anxiety always signals the need to make the unconscious conscious.

A young woman once approached me at a prayer meeting and asked if I would listen to a dream that had greatly troubled her some nights before. In this dream she was at a social function with a group of friends. All of a sudden an amorphous black figure stepped out of the crowd and sat on her. The figure literally sat on her chest with such force that she feared she would stop breathing. She remembered gasping for air and trying, unsuccessfully, to push the giant figure off. The harder she tried to get away, the heavier the figure became. She became terrified that she would die of asphyxiation.

In an effort to understand this dream, we talked about the significance of the giant, black figure. As I listened to the woman's associations with that figure, I saw clearly that the figure represented an emotionally stifling force that was causing her to feel constricted and beaten down. In clarifying the dream, I asked her whether she was aware of any ways in which she resembled this dark figure in her day-to-day dealings. At first, she did not accept the notion that this constricting personage resembled her in any way at all. On the contrary, she viewed herself as outgoing and emotionally very much at ease around others. She decided that she needed time to think about what the dream seemed to be saying to her.

A week later she came in with a glow on her face and told me that she had talked to a friend about the dream. In particular, she had shared how the dream seemed to be saying that, in some way, she was squeezing and constricting the life out of herself. She could not see how she was doing this. All she knew was that she felt anxious and upset whenever she thought about the dream. She reported to me how the friend had smiled at her reassuringly and sensitively revealed that she had been praying about this very matter.

For quite a long time the friend had been aware of an intense inner tension within this woman, especially during social activities. On the surface she would appear easygoing and sociable. However, the friend intuitively sensed a constricting tension underneath. As the woman and her friend talked, the origin of the tension became evident.

With much insight the woman acknowledged that she had been attempting to present a facade of ease and charm in order to hide the tension and fright that engulfed her during social activities. Her efforts to be very sweet and amiable had become more and more constricting and hurtful, until there was no sense of being herself. Indeed, she had been presenting this facade for so long that it took a great deal of effort just to bring to light the fact that it existed.

With insight provided by the dream, many memories surfaced. The woman recalled having been told repeatedly by both her mother and her father that she must always convey charm and confidenc: to others, so that people would not think of her as weak and try to take advantage of her. She remembered that, as a child, she had sought her mother's embrace in times of hardship — and that her mother would react by telling her that she needed to be strong, not dependent on hugs and kisses. As a result, she learned to present herself as confident, poised, and without a care in the world. Unfortunately, beneath this exterior lay great inner tension and insecurity.

In the woman's dream, her unconscious took the debilitating force within her and personified it as the dark figure that sat on her and literally squeezed the life out of her. As she worked through and became aware of the facets of this insight, she also requested to learn Christian meditation. Until now she had rebelled against the calm and ease produced by meditation. Unconsciously, she had thought that she must also present herself as poised and confident, without a care in the world, whenever she entered into her prayer time. She projected onto God the same feelings she had toward people in her life. As soon as she realized that she could allow herself to be calm and at ease in the presence of the Father, she experienced the tranquillity of being held by him in a way neither of her parents had ever held her.

Both from a Jungian perspective and a Christian perspective, our Father in heaven encompasses the living, nurturing, and containing qualities of a mother. In his paper entitled "The Energy of Warring and Combining Opposites: Problems for the Psychotic Patient and the Therapist in Achieving the Symbolic Situation," J.W.T. Redfearn, a Jungian analyst, comments:

> The mother-vessel-self archetype is a first coterminus with the cosmos and is at first relatively unbounded and undifferentiated. The containing and limiting of excitation is done by the actual mother. . . . Later still, the mother acquires more human dimensions and the containing function is located in the individual's own personal bodily self.

In order to understand the implications of these analytic words, we need to look more deeply into their meaning. When speaking of archetypes, Jungian theory is referring mainly to manners of acting, feeling, or believing that are inherent and innate within the individual and the society. Thus, in the context of the mother's activity of holding, each of the persons has an innate sense of holding and being held. Childbearing brings forth this innate capacity from within the woman. The child responds to tender holding and acknowledges the mother's embrace by feeling calmed and soothed. Any sensations of excitation, irritability, or anger in the child are contained by the mother's holding and soothing.

In describing the maternal archetype as being "at first relatively unbounded and undifferentiated" cosmically, Dr. Redfearn implies that within the cosmos a vast, undifferentiated, unbounded, and limitless resource of holding and caring exists. As Christians we know this resource to be the one who spoke in the Book of Isaiah:

Rejoice with Jerusalem, and be glad for her,
    all you who love her;
  rejoice with her in joy,
    all you who mourn over her;
  that you may suck and be satisfied
    with her consoling breasts;
  that you may drink deeply with delight
    from the abundance of her glory.
As one whom his mother comforts,
  so I will comfort you. . . .

(Isaiah 66:10-11,13)

3
LEARNING
TO MEDITATE

Introduction to Meditation

As we have read in Isaiah, our Father wishes to comfort us, to hold us in the divine embrace as his own children. By developing our capacity to meditate, we allow ourselves to be held by him who intimately cares for us. Saint Thomas Aquinas wrote of this intimacy:

So long as a thing exists, so long is God present to its being. But the being of a thing is that which is most intimate to it, it is that which most deeply resides in it, since being is the form of all that which it encloses. Hence God is in all things, and is intimately in them.

The Gospel of Jesus is a gospel of intimacy and calm. The challenge for the Christian is to open up inwardly to the calming power of Christ Jesus in the midst of an often frenzied world. I have met individuals who have tasted the intimacy and calm of his holding in meditation and yet fail to sustain its nurturance in their lives. The process of attuning ourselves to his holding calm does require discipline. Without the disciplined attention and regularity that meditation requires, its full sustenance and healing will not be internalized. When a person decides to approach and resolutely integrate meditation into a totally Christian life-style, then the sweet fruit of meditation will be tasted.

The Need for Formal Meditation

The Scriptures proclaim: *"Thou dost keep him in perfect peace, whose mind is stayed on thee. . . . "* (Isaiah 26:3) Keeping our minds and hearts stayed or focused on Jesus infers the necessity of establishing a way to do that. Once in a while I encounter someone who argues that if we truly live in union with God then our entire lives are a prayer, and so we have no need to set aside specific daily times to meditate. I have no doubt that some living saints walking on this earth may be in such constant communion with God that deciding on a specific time to meditate would be no different than going about their normal activities. So I suppose that if a person honestly senses an encompassing presence of God at all times then there would be no need to engage in formal meditation.

Quite honestly, though, I have met only one person in my lifetime whom I would regard as authentically, genuinely, continuously immersed in God's presence in a conscious way. When I met the man, he had already passed ninety years or more on this earth. His countenance communicated calm and vitality of spirit. His eyes seemed to shine with a penetrating light, as he related to me that since boyhood he had always had a personal and experiential knowledge of Jesus. As he would go about his daily activities, assisting his parents on their farm, he always consciously felt surrounded and filled with God. Later in his life he sensed an inner prompting to leave all that he had and go to the Himalaya Mountains, where he lived for forty years in a small hut or a cave.

In no way did he question the purpose in going to the Himalayas. He never had need to question his inner promptings; he knew them to be pure and guiding. I remember his sharing with me, ''I never question them, now that I think about it. I have never even thought of questioning them. As I have had strong inner promptings, I have always followed them. In doing this, fulfillment and blessing have been multiplied in me.''

As we talked about formal meditation, he remarked that, even though he did not find it necessary for himself, he could understand how necessary it would be for those living in the modern world. The peace of the Himalaya Mountains cultivated the constancy of God's experienced presence; the fast pace of modern living, on the other hand, acts to distract one from the presence of God. Because of this, regular times of reuniting with God's presence are needed to replenish the spirit.

My own conclusion is that explaining away the need for formal times of meditation on the basis that the living of life is one's prayer is more of a theoretical notion than a heartfelt experience. There are no two ways about it, the disciplining of the ego to practice meditation is hard work. It would be far easier to live under the intellectual and theoretical notion of God's presence being always with us — so why pray?

Truly, God is always with us. My concern lies in the fact that our presence may not always be with God. How can it be, living as we do in the midst of a distracting and fast-paced world?

A Case in Point

One woman determinedly confronted me on this matter. She told me with great conviction that she no longer needed to put aside time for meditation or prayer because she had grown so close to God that she continually felt aware of him. She said this after having practiced Christian meditation for a period of one year. I had no doubt, as I told her, that she had experienced a new nearness to him. She needed to remember, however, that this newly found closeness was the result of disciplined time spent with him in meditation.

Despite my exhortation, she decided to quit her daily meditation and just enjoy his constant being with her. Fortunately, God had blessed this woman with much humility. After one week she came to the church at which I was speaking and publicly told the group how important the disciplined usage of meditation was to her. She said that a few days without her time with the Lord had found her irritable and ill at ease about life. She no longer felt the inner desire to read the Scriptures. The presence of him who had been so near now was less clearly discernible. She summed up her story by saying, "I felt high and dry. I somehow knew that God had not moved away from me; I had moved away from him. When I began my daily times of meditation, I felt refreshed and reoriented. It was as if I had come home after having been away."

Thus, one's life-style and even personality characteristics influence meditation. The ninety-year-old monk I referred to noted that certain individuals seem to have natural meditative dispositions; others require more discipline in order to cultivate the meditative spirit. The critical factor in the practice of Christian meditation is the ability, natural or acquired, to experience the holding and soothing of the Father's embrace.

Personality Characteristics and
the Capacity to Meditate

In planning my dissertation research I decided to inquire into the effect of Christian meditation on various personality characteristics. One of the areas of investigation concerned the possible effects of the practice of meditation on intrinsic and extrinsic personality orientations. Intrinsically oriented religious individuals are those who engage in the practice of their faith out of a sense of personal inspiration and conviction. Extrinsically religious persons attend church activities primarily because of the social nature of the event. Church activities and worship services attract them mainly because of the opportunity to be with friends and acquaintances. One of my hypotheses stated that meditation would cause a shifting of extrinsic personality orientations more toward intrinsic motivations in religious life.

My hypothesis did not bear out. Meditation did not have the anticipated effect because the individuals who voluntarily participated in the study were already intrinsically oriented in their Christian life. It seems that extrinsically oriented individuals do not have the same attraction toward meditation as do intrinsically motivated ones. This finding does not suggest that only intrinsically motivated persons can benefit from meditation. As a matter of fact, other studies have shown that extrinsically oriented persons would profit a great deal from meditation. For instance, some studies reveal that extrinsic individuals rely to a great degree on making a favorable impression on others. Much of their incessant activity centers on impressing others and learning how to function in the "in" group. Needless to say, this creates much inward stress. For such people the only relief from stress comes from finally achieving social recognition of one sort or another.

Learning the art of meditation helps these people to experience, perhaps for the first time, that calmness and relaxation may be brought about through inner means. They begin to understand that authentic peace and fulfillment come from a state of inner attunement rather than from social approval. And what can make a tremendous impact on them psychologically is the further discovery that the ability to experience calm comes from their own inner resources. Typically, this personal revelation causes their sense of self-esteem to be greatly enhanced. What they used to think depended on others is now experienced as emerging from the depths of the self.

Personality Characteristics and Meditation

In order to understand the interplay of personality characteristics and meditation, it might be helpful to look at a few general personality trends, their psychological dynamics and manifestations, and their influence on development of the capacity to meditate. Throughout this discussion, remember that general personality trends only approximate actual human behavior. No one person exactly fits any of the descriptions. Nevertheless, being informed about a general trend that may be similar to our way of functioning psychologically and interpersonally may help us understand why we act the way we do. It may also help us realize that we are not alone in all of this. It is particularly important to note that, in meditation, some people have an easy time while others find the discipline difficult. Knowing that our individual personality makeup influences our response to meditation helps to alleviate concern in this area.

The hard-driving personality. To begin with, contemporary psychology recognizes a definite personality type that maintains a furor of activity and daily tensions. Dr. Edgar Wilson, in the book *Staying Healthy Without Medicine,* has referred to these individuals as hard-driving and aggressive. Often, these people find it quite difficult, if not impossible, to relax. They were brought up with the belief that hard work is the most important part of life, a belief that has caused them to develop into exacting and perfectionistic people who are driven to succeed.

Various physical and biological traits accompany individuals in this group. Because they usually eat on the run during the day and then settle down to an evening meal rich in fats and calories, excess weight is a serious problem. Also, they depend on large amounts of coffee and sweets to maintain energy, thereby inviting other physical complications. Illnesses that characteristically plague these hard-driving persons include high blood pressure, migraine headaches, angina pectoris, heart attacks, strokes, ulcers and stomach troubles, severe menstrual cramps, bronchitis, emphysema, and alcohol problems linked with severe outbursts of anger.

Psychologically and interpersonally, these men and women constantly seek new challenges. They feel that they can overcome all obstacles by sheer willpower. They thrive on dominating others and exerting power over them. Rather than listen attentively or empathically to others, they prefer to talk and control conversations authoritatively.

As to the effect of this personality type on development of the capacity to meditate, I have found that typically there is resistance to the calm and quiet. Individuals complain that they feel pressured to get up and do something. One man told me that thoughts race through his mind saying, "You gotta go, gotta go and get the work done." The pressure to work interferes with the seemingly passive acceptance of calm.

Among these people I have also found the misconception that merely putting in the prescribed amount of time is equivalent to meditating. A businessman admitted that he, quite unconsciously, would open his eyes and begin to think about business transactions. Fifteen minutes later he would see that his time for meditation had passed, so he would get up and continue with the work of the day. Convincing oneself that putting in the time in the appropriate place qualifies as meditation is illusory and steals away the potential benefit of meditation.

Even though hyperalert and aggressive qualities may be of some help in attaining business and professional recognition, their habitual use needs to be tempered for the sake of one's physical, psychological, and spiritual well-being. In the words of the Epistle to the Romans, if those of us who are hard-driven are going to pursue anything, *"Let us then pursue what makes for peace and for mutual upbuilding."* (Romans 14:19)

The following guidelines will act to temper the hurtful aspects of the hard-driving personality:

1. At intervals during each day, try to relax and be still in the presence of God. Let these be short times of awareness of God's presence throughout the day.
2. Exercise each day in a noncompetitive way, such as by taking a long, quiet walk with someone you feel close to.
3. Be moderate in eating habits, especially at the evening meal.
4. Discipline yourself to listen, for at least a full minute each day, with undivided attention, to your spouse or someone else who is close to you.

These guidelines will help the hard-driving person to be less forceful in daily living. A young businessman once questioned this approach. He let me know that he did not want to be less forceful because that implied a less intense life-style. He enjoyed intensity in his work, in his relationships, and in his recreation. The problem for him could be seen in the fact that, in each of these areas, intensity and forcefulness had been confused.

As we pursued the matter, it became obvious that his force-fulness caused many problems. The women he dated often complained of his being very opinionated, boastful, and generally intrusive. Secretly, he prided himself in this criticism since he believed that few people had the strength of character not to be intimidated by him. Clients in his work also complained, sometimes to his manager, that he would not quit hounding them about matters that had been settled and decided. It was as if he respected no one or nothing. It was only through genuine self-reflection that his hidden yet blatantly destructive disrespect for others surfaced to awareness.

Through this realization the young man gradually disentangled himself from his devastating manner of relating. He started to implement some of the above guidelines. Rather than brag about himself to his girl friends, he now felt free enough to listen to what interested them. With others, he found that he could easily enjoy taking a walk through the mountains as opposed to beating them in sports. Applying the guidelines permitted him to be more receptive to meditation. In experiencing the profundity of meditation, he realized that forcefulness has little to do with true intensity. Intensity does not relate to force. Real intensity echoes the saying, "In quietness and peace lies my strength." Disentangling ourselves from the force and current of the world in the depths of meditation, as Jesus did in the desert, stirs within us an intensity of faith. As the Christian mystic Louis de Blois affirmed:

> This takes place where a pure, humble, and resigned soul, burning with ardent love, is carried above itself by the grace of God, and through the brilliancy of the divine light shining on the mind it loses all consideration and distinction of things . . . and is transformed and changed into Him, as iron placed in the fire is changed into fire, without ceasing to be iron.

The anxious personality. The hard-driving personality entangles himself in the forcefulness of the world. Another type of personality, referred to as the anxious personality, is more prone toward getting entangled in patterns of anxiety and constant worry in daily living. Family members raised in an anxious environment frequently show mood swings and feelings of uncertainty. Prolonged inner stress may manifest itself in continual concerns about health, although no physical illnesses may ever be diagnosed.

Worriers typically ingest great quantities of medication and vitamins in order to combat vague chronic pains that can seldom be attributed to physical causes. In an attempt to relieve these pains, alcohol and drugs may be used, even to the point of abuse. Other physical problems commonly include cirrhosis, chronic lung disease, and various types of accidents.

Unfortunately, rather than turn to others for help, these people withdraw from close interpersonal relationships. It seems that their doubts and fears regarding self-worth keep them distanced from others lest someone should find them out. Anxiety and depression are frequent psychological symptoms.

The Scriptures offer assistance in reminding the Christian with this type of personality style that *"we have the mind of Christ."* (1 Corinthians 2:16) Rather than permit ourselves to be tormented by worry upon worry, it is important to begin to exercise our capacity for self-control of thoughts (Galatians 5:23). A helpful way of doing this is to identify the energy-draining worry concretely, learn what the fear may be trying to teach, and then decide how the situation causing worry can be productively resolved. Thereafter, whenever this worry comes to mind, literally tell it to *stop*. Then begin to dwell on the productive resolution of the problem, reinforcing the positive outcome in your mind.

The Case of a Worried Nun

A nun who had been in the convent for many years and excelled in the service of her parish was being honored at a banquet. Many weeks beforehand, she began worrying about the speech she was to give. Fretting over it kept her up at night and even stole her appetite. She shared this with me one evening after a prayer meeting. Together we identified the worry as fear of appearing foolish before the others in the parish. She could almost hear the words going through her mind, ''You're going to make a fool of yourself right in front of everyone.''

As we explored what this fear might be trying to teach her, she became aware of a secret pride beneath the fear. She felt proud that out of all the nuns in the parish, she had been chosen to be honored. But could she, who was being so honored, ever appear as less than perfect? The humility she had so often taught seemed to be far from her. For this occasion she had thought only of relying on her own wit, wisdom, and skill to carry her through. It had not occurred to her that it was only because of God and service to him that she was being honored. Fear was attempting to bring her to a point of humility before the One whom she served. As she realized her complete dependence on him and acknowledged this pride, she felt a sense of release. Later she told me that whenever the thought of appearing foolish entered her mind, she would say to herself, "In all ways I will humble myself before my Lord. He is my all." As a result she did well in her speech and felt quite at peace throughout the ceremony.

Frank's Case

Frank was a young man in his early twenties who had just graduated from business school. He was in the process of job hunting. Usually, whenever he had an interview, he would begin to worry the night before, focusing on all the reasons why he wouldn't get the job. The result would be a severe headache.

Frank identified his worry as a fear that he would disappoint his family, especially his father. For a long time he had thought that his family considered him lazy and not committed to his work. They seemed convinced that he had finished college through his ability to take tests and pass them rather than through dedication to the task at hand.

Frank candidly admitted to me that he harbored a sense of grandiosity because of his effortless academic accomplishments. He realized, however, that if he approached any interview with this cocksure attitude, disaster would result. The fear warned him of this.

With this new understanding of his fear, Frank recognized that the energy that had formerly turned into fear could motivate him to prepare for interviews. He found that when he was prepared, fear no longer plagued him. Whenever the thought of failure entered his mind, he firmly said, "Stop!" He then focused on this line from Scripture: *"I can do all things in him who strengthens me."* (Philippians 4:13)

Why is it necessary to tell thoughts to stop? After all, it would seem to make logical sense that if we learn the root cause of troubling emotion then the emotion should cease — and so should the attitude or thought that caused it. This seems sensible, but in real life unwanted thoughts or attitudes have a way of inviting themselves back. When a person has been dwelling on a thought for a long time, it may take firmness to change the habit. It takes time and attentiveness to dissolve a pattern of negative thinking.

Frank soon noticed that his attitude had changed from cockiness to a realistic confidence that resulted from adequate preparation. He projected to others such a different countenance that he was hired by the personnel director of a large computer firm. His realistic confidence conveyed an interpersonal ease that the director appreciated. Whenever I saw Frank from then on, he always told me what a difference it made in him to dwell on the positive power of scriptural verses.

Along with all of this, Frank experienced a new freedom in meditation. During meditation, worries no longer dominated his mental activity. In fact, he discovered that during the deep relaxation he found in meditation, suppressed feelings surfaced that he was able to learn from. At the end of his meditations, if he found himself aware of a previously hidden emotion or thought, he would make a note of it in his journal. Doing so helped him to sort out the meaning of the thought or feeling, to see what it was trying to teach him. As he acquired the self-knowledge that the emotions wished to convey, it became unnecessary for these emotions to return. A quality of clear-mindedness characterized his meditations.

The overcontrolled personality. Like Frank, many persons tend to suppress emotions rather than to experience them and learn what they wish to convey. But there is another personality type that engages in emotional suppression *habitually*. The psalmist expresses the consequence of emotional denial and suppression thus:

> *When I declared not my sin, my body wasted away*
> *through my groaning all day long.*
> *For day and night thy hand was heavy upon me;*
> *my strength was dried up as by the heat of summer.*
> (Psalm 32:3-4)

With this type of personality pattern, feelings are strictly controlled, even denied. Real feelings are hidden away. So are desires and wishes. In this way a person feels protected from ever having to confront failure or criticism. Parents who are like this frequently tell their children things like, ''You are selfish if you talk about your own needs.'' These parents may even convey to their children the notion that the world is a hurtful and dangerous place. With this kind of attitude, a person is constantly living in fear of hurting others or of being hurt.

Individuals of this type literally suffer bodily pangs of overcontrol. Because of the tension developed in maintaining such control, muscles in the neck and shoulders seem always to be braced and tight, even to the point of causing pain. Such constant muscle tension and contraction results in feelings of physical fatigue and a sense of being bound up. As a result of the muscle spasms, muscular fibrosis and degeneration of joints may ensue. Physical problems include low back pain, chronic fatigue, tension headaches, high blood pressure, arthritis, and heart disease. When these persons choose to exercise, the exercise frequently involves self-defense activities such as boxing, wrestling, and playing defense on a football team.

Once again, the psalmist suggests an insightful approach to this kind of conflict:

> *I acknowledged my sin to thee,*
>   *and I did not hide my iniquity;*
> *I said, "I will confess my transgressions to the LORD";*
>   *then thou didst forgive the guilt of my sin.*
>
> (Psalm 32:5)

The psalmist encourages us to express ourselves. We need not think that he is referring solely to suppressed sins. Strict suppression of our deepest feelings and needs is also a cause of inner heaviness and depression. Learning to take time aside daily to share our feelings with someone we feel we can trust is crucial here. Allowing our feelings to be released generates a tremendous sense of relief so that in unison with the psalmist we, too, can proclaim:

Be glad in the LORD, and rejoice, O righteous,
and shout for joy, all you upright in heart!
(Psalm 32:11)

The tendency in the overcontrolled person is to push away troublesome feelings that emerge at the end of meditation. Depending on the extent and duration of the emotional suppression, memories of past hurtful relationships may surface. When these come to awareness they need to be heeded. If the old memories or feelings are very strong or even overwhelming, psychological care should be sought. Sometimes it is only within the containing relationship of psychotherapy that buried conflicts can be resolved. But meditation, by itself, frequently provides people with sufficient inner security to face feelings and conflicts and to resolve them unassisted. Many times the touch of God's presence in meditation causes the most hardened of hearts to melt away in his love. The mystic Richard Rolle wrote profoundly about this unity in God's love:

O love everlasting, inflame my soul to love God, that nothing may burn in me but His embraces. . . . Come into my heart and fill it with Thy most excellent sweetness. Inebriate my mind with the hot wine of Thy sweet love, that forgetting all evils and all scornful visions and imaginations, and having Thee alone, I may be glad and rejoice in Jesus my God.

The Meditative Setting

It is too easy to suppose that meditation is so simple to do that no preparation for it is necessary. The truth is, preparation is just as important as meditation itself. We can characterize the preparation in the words of John the Baptizer, *"Make straight the way of the Lord."* (John 1:23)

The phrase *meditative setting* refers to the ways in which we prepare our bodies and our physical surroundings for meditation. First of all, it is important to consider our *bodily disposition* when we enter into meditation. Meditation relaxes and settles us. There-fore, it is important that no food or stimulant be allowed to inhibit the effect of the meditative experience. Eating causes the body to be tense and ready to digest the food. Eating before meditating affects the experience. It is always best not to meditate within one hour after food has been taken. Stimulants such as cola, coffee, and tea are best avoided for a two-hour period before meditation. During meditation our bodies need to be able to cooperate with the process of relaxation without being inhibited by digesting food or being otherwise stimulated physiologically.

The *place of meditation,* also, greatly influences our meditative experience. A room should be chosen that is relatively quiet and away from the normal course of daily activity. This helps the meditator not to be distracted by other activities in the house. I have known parents to post on their bedroom door a small sign reading "Quiet, Please." This reminds the rest of the family to be respect-ful of each member's quiet time in meditation.

During meditation the room should be only dimly lit. Also, organizing and straightening up the room, if need be, helps to provide an atmosphere of peace and quiet. All such physical preparations assist the meditator to acquire a sense of settledness and calm prior to meditation.

It is important to consider the *position of the body* in meditation. Most of us are accustomed to kneeling while in prayer. Among experienced meditators, however, the consensus seems to be that kneeling does not help. In the kneeling position the body becomes uncomfortable and ill at ease. It is best to sit in a chair that allows the spine to remain as nearly erect as possible. A straight spine, together with comfortable seating, helps the meditator to relax for an extended period of time.

It is also helpful to loosen shoes or tight clothing. The more we allow the body to feel comfortable before meditation, the smoother the transition into meditation will be.

During meditation we sometimes need to change positions, scratch an itch, or even sneeze. None of these activities hampers the meditative experience. Simply allow meditation to occur as naturally as possible. Meditation is not meant to be a rigorously disciplined exercise but a time of calm and peace.

When beginning to meditate, it is helpful to have a quiet clock nearby. This allows the meditator to gently open his or her eyes slightly now and then to check the time. Loud noises tend to shock the relaxed nervous system of the meditator, so it is best not to have an alarm go off during meditation. If the telephone rings or someone knocks at the door, it is helpful to pause for a moment before answering; meditation should never be interrupted suddenly. When rising, the meditator should move slowly and quietly to enable the body to maintain an ease of transition from the relaxed meditative state to the more active state.

Once meditation is formally completed, the meditator will experience maximum benefit from it if a time of transition is provided for. The best way to accomplish this is to gently open the eyes, reflect upon one's state of relaxation, and gently move the hands by rubbing them together or by rubbing them against the face as when awakening from sleep. Remaining seated for a minute or so after meditation and allowing the thoughts to return to everyday activities helps to integrate the sense of relaxation and calm into the normal activities of the day.

"He who fails to prepare is preparing to fail." Even though there is no such thing as failure or success in meditation, preparing for it helps us to experience depth and tranquillity, so that our words echo the words of the psalmist:

> *He who dwells in the shelter of the Most High,*
> *who abides in the shadow of the Almighty,*
> *will say to the LORD, "My refuge and my fortress;*
> *my God, in whom I trust."*

(Psalm 91:1-2)

To sum up, the general guidelines for meditation are these:

1. Avoid eating or using stimulants such as coffee, tea, or cola for an hour or two before meditation.
2. Choose a quiet setting in which to meditate.
3. Meditate in a comfortable position.
4. Allow for slight changes in body position during meditation. They may be needed and should not be avoided.

5. If interrupted during meditation, take time for smooth transition.
6. Use a quiet clock that can be looked at periodically by opening the eyes only slightly.
7. When finishing meditation, have an interval of a minute or so to sit in the same position with eyes open in order to adjust to external stimulation.

The Meditative Attitude

"For God alone my soul waits in silence." (Psalm 62:1) In depicting the meditative attitude, the psalmist describes a condition of nonforcefulness and quiet. Nonforcefulness means that the meditator in no way presses or stresses himself or herself during meditation. It is as if we enter into meditation simply to attune ourselves to the name of Jesus that is constantly being uttered by the Holy Spirit within. Our duty, therefore, lies simply in becoming aware of his name occurring within us.

The meditative attitude of gentleness and awareness creates the climate in which the soul can breathe from the very purity of breath coming from the being of the Father. As the Scriptures assert, *"In him we live and move and have our being."* (Acts 17:28) As naturally as our bodies breathe in and out, the name of Jesus can continue within the heart of the meditator effortlessly, spontaneously, purely.

As the focus of meditation, the name of Jesus will carry on by itself. It is as if the meditator permits the meditation to go on without interruption, only observing it as it takes place. Rather than engage in meditation, we attune ourselves to it. The process occurs naturally. The only effort involved is that of being aware.

A young stockbroker with whom I was working in psychotherapy commented about the relief he felt as he began to learn how to meditate. A need to be superior in his business had forced him to perform under great pressure. Inadvertently, he had transferred the pressure into his relationship with God. He somehow had acquired the notion that he could never do enough to be really pleasing to God. As he learned to cultivate effortless awareness of the name of

Jesus, he experienced a great psychological release. This pressured businessman grew to know the deep freedom that comes from being present to God, being aware of his presence through the uttering of his name.

In a sense, I am speaking of flowing with the name of Jesus. As the meditator practices meditation with the Jesus Prayer, the name of Jesus acquires a life of its own within the meditator. During formal times of meditation, but also during the course of the day, the name of Jesus will come to mind. His name seems to flow through the mind periodically throughout the day. These moments touch the meditator with a remembrance and rekindling of calm.

A close friend of mine, a Benedictine monk of many years, told me how the name of Jesus often touches him during his day. He recalled how in the middle of a conversation with someone the previous day the name of Jesus had come to mind and refreshed him. He also told of being busily involved in preparing dinner for the monastery and, in a brief moment, being consumed with the love of Jesus through the recollection of his name. "I was just standing here in the midst of pots and pans when I felt him come to me — like a burning presence within my heart and all around me. Can you imagine that in the middle of doing such ordinary work he would come to me and let me know how much he loves me? It's not that I heard him say anything; he just let me know in a very definite way, without any words at all, how much I meant to him. It was as though he hugged me and embraced me. I was intoxicated with the love of Jesus while preparing dinner and scrubbing pots and pans!"

The Meditative Silence

. . . the LORD is in his holy temple;
let all the earth keep silence before him.
(Habakkuk 2:20)

A young man described his experience of meditative silence in the following manner: "It is 4:00 A.M. I am awakened by the sound of monastic bells calling the religious community to prayer. As I peer from the window of my room, I see the faithful walking to the chapel, lighting the darkness with their lanterns. As I join them, a deep silence surrounds me. At that moment the entire earth seems to keep silent before him.''

During meditation this sort of silence embraces our spirit. Within the silence can be found the presence of him who is called the All in All. All of him envelops the entirety of our being.

The silent awareness of him does not exclude the surfacing of thoughts. These thoughts need not interfere with the meditative silence. In fact, some research has noted that thoughts during meditation release tension. The thought of a given event during the day releases the tension associated with that event. I do not mean to say that we should dwell on thoughts, but only that thoughts are not necessarily counterproductive of meditation. When thoughts come to mind, we can allow them to pass like a cloud through the sky. They may be treated as a natural occurrence, much like the tension release of a muscle that jerks. Permitting thoughts to pass away and resuming focus on the name of Jesus maximize the depth of the experience of meditative silence.

So it is that during the meditative silence the name of Jesus need not be concentrated on. A gentle focusing on his name is all that is required. When thoughts come to mind, the meditator allows the thoughts to pass away and gently returns to focusing on the name. As we return to his name, all thoughts will vanish and be washed away, for *"at the name of Jesus every knee should bow, in heaven and on earth and under the earth, and every tongue confess that Jesus Christ is Lord, to the glory of God the Father."* (Philippians 2:10-11)

Learning to Meditate: Children

One afternoon a very wise friend of mine and I were talking about the capacity of children to meditate. This friend was particularly blessed in that he had experientially known the presence of God, moment by moment, since his childhood years. He said, ''God surrounded and filled me. As a child I was always aware of his presence.'' Our discussion led us to conclude that early spiritual training sets the foundation for later spiritual life.

My friend described a form of meditation that children can use and that helps to build a foundation of firm spiritual development. The technique is referred to as a "moving meditation." A child, either alone or with a parent, paces back and forth over a designated area and recites the Jesus Prayer in a whispering manner. Either a rosary or a set of Jesus beads helps the child to attend to the process of meditation. On each bead of the rosary the words, "Lord, Jesus" are pronounced prayerfully, slowly, and deliberately. Similarly, with Jesus beads — a rosary-like formation of one hundred beads — the name of Jesus is pronounced on each bead.

After learning of this type of meditation, one parent initiated the practice of taking his daughter to their backyard each morning to pray and meditate. They would walk up and back about twenty-five paces in their garden, reciting the Jesus Prayer. The time spent together became not only a time of prayer but also a time of nurturing their relationship.

Morning meditation should respect a child's limitations. Children cannot engage in tasks for long periods without interruption or lapse of concentration. For example, meditating for fifteen to twenty minutes would prove much too cumbersome for a child of twelve to fourteen years of age. A shorter period — up to five or ten minutes — is more realistic.

A young husband and wife with whom I was working in marital therapy were experiencing difficulty trying to teach their children how to pray. Whenever prayer was mentioned the children would squirm and fight the idea. The father would call the children to pray in the evening when they were watching their favorite television program; he would turn off the TV and announce that it was time for prayer. The family would then read a passage from Scripture and say the rosary on their knees. Prayer time involved severe reprimands to the boys, six- and eight-year-olds, who were frequently caught making faces and poking each other. The problem kept occurring and the parents could not understand why.

The fact of the matter was that the parents expected the children to be models of perfect behavior for thirty entire minutes of prayer. One of the boys told me, "At least at Mass it's not so boring. We're standing up and sitting down, shaking hands with each other, singing songs, going to communion, and stuff like that. At home it's so boring. All Dad does is tell us to concentrate on what we are doing and settle down.''

I suggested that the father spend five or ten minutes in daily prayer time with each of the boys separately. I taught him how to use the walking meditation, focusing on the name of Jesus. Since the actual meditation would last only three or four minutes, both he and his son could use the rest of the time to talk about the feelings and experiences of the day.

This plan worked out so well that the boys actually began to look forward to their "time with Dad." Needless to say, playing football or baseball, and even going out for an occasional ice cream cone, contributed greatly to the relationship and to the eagerness with which the boys began looking forward to prayer. Time with Dad and time with God proved increasingly enjoyable.

Children have an innate curiosity about the spiritual, as well as an attraction toward it. Notice the attentiveness that children exhibit whenever angels, spirits, or the supranatural are being discussed. I remember that when I was a youngster in parochial school the entire class would look forward to visits by our parish priest, who would tell us about things like angels, devils, and miracles. When we offer prayer and meditation as ways of being in contact with the God of the universe, who created all spiritual creatures, children respond. Their appetite is whetted for further spiritual experience.

A young woman whom I was treating in psychotherapy admitted an intense desire for prayer that began when she was a child. She recalled the devotion of her parents, especially the devotion of her mother, whom she often observed reading the Bible and praying. She remembered that sitting on her father's lap and talking with him about heaven, hell, God, and angels was a regular occurrence.

When the young woman moved away from home, the busy atmosphere of college life and various social activities pulled her away from spiritual things. She came into psychotherapy in order to find her way back to her spiritual center. After spending some time focusing on releasing and resolving many feelings that stormed within her as the result of homesickness, I introduced her to the Jesus Prayer. In her words, ''I took to the Jesus Prayer like a fish to water. It rekindled the love of the spiritual life within me. It was the same feeling I had had as a child watching my mother at prayer or sitting on my father's lap and talking about God.'' In essence, the foundation for her later spiritual experience had been laid by her parents' cultivation of a loving and relaxed kind of Christian spirituality within the home.

In many parents there is a tendency to try to force faith onto their children. When this route is taken, neither parents nor children can help but experience a great deal of hostility and animosity toward each other. Such hostility toward parents is translated into a definite repulsion toward God. In the child's mind God is the cause of this forcing and fighting. Forcing faith forces children away from God.

Cultivating an interest in and a desire for spiritual experience through example is the most powerful motivator for children. In fact, children will do as you do, not as you tell them. As they observe the love that a life of prayer generates between mother and father, as they witness the supranatural answering of prayer, as they feel the peace and calm that come from meditating with their parents, then will children naturally seek the spiritual experience and fulfillment that comes from encountering Jesus daily in meditation.

Learning to Meditate: Adults

John, a young attorney who had recently attended one of my seminars on meditation, related to me how the practice of meditation was both rewarding and difficult for him. He said, ''You made it sound too easy. I have been trying to meditate every day this week, but it's difficult to find time to just sit there in a state of calm and relaxation, focusing on the name of Jesus. It's hard to take time from a busy schedule to do anything that seems so nonproductive; however, I must admit that once I have completed my meditation, I feel much more calm and refreshed after experiencing the presence of God.''

Calmness and refreshment characterize meditation; however, throughout the years that I have been teaching on meditation, people have always commented not only on the benefits of meditation but also on the discipline of establishing a daily time to meditate. So, in all fairness, it behooves me to preface my discussion of adult meditation by noting that together with the spiritual growth toward calm and peace there also exists the challenge of spiritual discipline, especially with regard to time.

Here I am reminded of Jesus' words, " . . . *unless a grain of wheat falls into the earth and dies, it remains alone; but if it dies, it bears much fruit. He who loves his life loses it, and he who hates his life in this world will keep it for eternal life."* (John 12:24-25) Allotting time for personal prayer is, in a manner of speaking, dying to self. The duties and pleasures of the day seek to impose themselves and take complete priority over prayer and meditation. Our responsibilities need to be fulfilled; but, all too often, we include in our daily routines some activities that are not altogether necessary. Rather than watch one hour of television nightly we may need to limit ourselves to one-half hour in order to spend thirty minutes in meditation. We may need to realize that some household duties can actually be left until tomorrow. Dying to ourselves for a few minutes each day, by setting aside the cares of the world and entering into prayer, will bless us with a life of greater calm and peace.

In addition to the guidelines provided earlier in this chapter, the following can be used by adults to learn the art of Christian meditation:

1. Sit quietly in a comfortable position.
2. Close your eyes.
3. Breathe through your nose. Become aware of your breathing. As you breathe in, focus on "Lord." As you breathe out, focus silently on "Jesus." Breathe in, "Lord . . ."; breathe out, "Jesus . . ."; and so on. Breathe easily and naturally.
4. Do not worry about whether you are successful in achieving a deep state of relaxation. Maintain a passive attitude and permit relaxation to occur at its own pace. When distracting thoughts occur, allow them to pass away by not dwelling on

them, and return to repeating "Lord . . . , Jesus." With practice, relaxation should come with little effort.

5. Continue for fifteen minutes. You may open your eyes to check on the time, but do not use an alarm.
6. When finished, sit quietly for a minute or so with your eyes open in order to reorient yourself to the external world. Stand up slowly.
7. Practice the techniques twice daily, but not within two hours after any meal.

In my experience it usually takes six to eight weeks before the full impact of Christian meditation can be felt. Some of the research reveals that individuals feel greatly relaxed immediately after beginning meditation. After the first meditation, such physical signs as respiration, peripheral temperature, and blood lactate level are positively affected; however, despite those immediate physical signs of relaxation, the meditator's concept of himself or herself as a more relaxed and calm person requires a greater amount of time to take hold. The meditator actually begins to realize that he or she is a more relaxed and calm person somewhere around the sixth to eighth week of meditation.

The fact that a change in self-image comes only after six to eight weeks of meditation informs us that psychological and spiritual growth requires both patience and discipline. As adults, reorientation of our lives, so as to include a scheduled time for prayer, may not be easy; but personal spiritual depth will increase only as the Lord of Life is encountered in a regular and constant manner. Engaged in day by day, for fifteen minutes twice each day, meditation will build in the meditator a richness of spiritual experience that will lead to a profound knowledge of Jesus. With patience and persistance our relationship with him develops so that we will, over time, internalize the very essence of Jesus' character — peace.

Learning to Meditate: Families

Since the family provides the basis from which all other relationships are formed, the development of peace and calm within the family is of crucial importance. If a child experiences peace within the family, the chances will be greater that when he or she begins a new family it too will carry on the tradition of peace. Generation after generation, families either pass on fear and anxiety or bequeath peace and a harmonious, God-filled life to their posterity.

Not long ago I was approached by a very upset father who frantically complained that he could no longer manage his six-year-old son. The son would defy him, blatantly defy him. If the father would make a request, the boy would be sure not to comply. The boy seemed rebellious and very, very angry.

I encouraged the father to bring the family together for a time of meditation with the Jesus Prayer. I told him to place his hand gently on his son during meditation. Frequently, the depth of relaxation experienced during meditation permits the natural love of parents for their children to surface; I encouraged the father to leave his hand on his son's shoulder until he felt that love surface.

A few weeks later the father told me about an unexpected change that occurred in his family. The mighty effect of meditation had caused him to feel a new love for his son. In fact, he had begun to realize that much of his son's defiance and anger was caused by his own secretly and subtly felt anger toward the boy. For reasons stemming from his own past, the father had been resenting the child. Without the father's awareness, the resentment had been conveyed to the son in such small ways as a sharp glance for no reason, a cutting word, or a refusal to grant permission without giving an adequate explanation. All of this had motivated anger in the boy, who thought that his father did not love him. As the father began to show love for the son, their relationship became one of enjoying each other, and mutual love emerged as the result of the time spent together in the quiet and calm of meditation.

The following guidelines are recommended for the family wishing to participate together in meditation:

1. Find a quiet place in the home to sit together for a period of time. This could be the family den or living room, or any place where the noise of the telephone or doorbell will not disturb the quiet of meditation.

2. Have each family member sit in a comfortable position. Some of the younger ones (under twelve years of age) may find that lying on the floor is the most relaxing position for them. Older children and adults will probably find that sitting in a chair provides them with maximum comfort.

3. If this is the first family meditation, the parents should explain to the children why this time of prayer is going to be an important part of family life. The parents should emphasize that it is a time to relax together. Because it is very frustrating to be torn away from an enjoyable activity, the best time for family prayer is at a designated time in the evening when homework, television watching, and all other activities are over. For most families the ideal time is about ten minutes before bedtime, when other activities will not be interfered with; then no one will resent the time of prayer.

4. One of the parents can begin the meditation by intoning the Jesus Prayer. That is, the words "Lord, . . . Jesus" will be chanted according to a particular tone set by the leader. The parents can explain to the children that chanting helps them to concentrate more easily on the Jesus Prayer.

5. Keep in mind that for families, time spent in prayer can reach a point of diminishing returns. Too long a period causes the children to become restless, so that prayer becomes a chore. Five to ten minutes seems to be an adequate amount of time for most families to meditate together.

6. As in individual meditation, do not worry about success at meditation. That concern only distracts the members from being at ease. The only way to fail at meditation with the Jesus Prayer is not to do it. It is best to maintain a passive attitude and allow relaxation to occur at its own pace. Encourage family members not to dwell on distracting thoughts; simply allow thoughts to pass away like the clouds passing through the sky and return to focusing on the name of Jesus. The more the family practices meditation, the easier it will be to relax.

4

THE TEMPLE
OF INNER CALM

The Body and the Power of Jesus

*Do you not know that your body is a temple of the Holy Spirit
within you, which you have from God? You are not your own;
you were bought with a price. So glorify God in your body.*
(1 Corinthians 6:19-20)

Adults, children, and families are called spiritually, emotionally, and physically to experience the calming and healing effects
of a daily inner encounter with Jesus. Spirits are meant to be lifted
toward him. Emotions can be soothed by the touch of his presence.
Bodies can be healed and calmed by the Prince of Peace who
resides in the innermost part of the temple of our soul.

In his First Letter to the Corinthians, Saint Paul emphasizes the
fact that our bodies are meant to come under the total influence of
the Holy Spirit. Our bodies act as temples for the indwelling Holy
Spirit, thanks to the fact that we were bought with a price, with the
blood of Christ Jesus. Because Jesus suffered, died, and rose again
from the dead, the human body can begin to manifest the healing
and the power that is available directly from the Spirit of Jesus.

Our bodies are the temple of the Holy Spirit. Saint Paul says:
'' . . . *our commonwealth is in heaven, and from it we await a
Savior, the Lord Jesus Christ, who will change our lowly body to*

be like his glorious body, by the power which enables him even to subject all things to himself." (Philippians 3:20-21) This verse implies that, in changing our bodies, we can experience an outward transformation away from the principle of sin and toward being under the total influence of the Holy Spirit. Granted, the transformation will not be complete until we see Jesus face-to-face; this life is meant to be a gradual growing toward the total yielding of ourselves to the influence of the Holy Spirit. But as we move away from sin and toward the Holy Spirit, even our physical bodies can experience the power and rejuvenation of the Holy Spirit.

Effects on the Physical Body

So then it is no longer that I do it, but sin which dwells within me. For I know that nothing good dwells within me, that is, in my flesh. I can will what is right, but I cannot do it. . . . Now if I do what I do not want, it is no longer I that do it, but sin which dwells within me. . . . Who will deliver me from this body of death? Thanks be to God through Jesus Christ our Lord! So then, I of myself serve the law of God with my mind, but with my flesh I serve the law of sin. (Romans 7:17-18,20,24-25)

In this passage of his Letter to the Romans, Paul notes that even though our mind and our spirit desire to serve the living Christ, our flesh may still experience the effects of sin. This truth is manifested by a variety of physical discomforts and ailments, even serious illness. I do not mean to say that all physical ailments and problems result from an individual's personal sinfulness. I am saying only that as a result of the collective sinfulness in this world, from which we are not yet completely liberated, we may be subject at times to physical discomfort and ailments. It is through our Lord Jesus Christ that we are delivered from the effects of death and sin on our body. Therefore, as we deepen our relationship with the Holy Spirit, Jesus, and the Father, we will gradually experience peace and liberation of this body from death.

Saint Paul speaks of the human body as a "vile body." In literal Greek the words refer to the body's humble origin in humiliation through the transgression of Adam. Rather than being in its original state as created in the image and likeness of God, the body now experiences the humiliation of sin. Because of this, humankind is prone to sickness and disease.

Jesus fashions this humiliated body to be like his glorious body. Once again, the original Greek connotation of Paul's words is that this fashioning of the outward body, so as to be like the glorious body of Jesus, serves as an outward expression of an inner nature. As our inner spirits reflect the Spirit of Jesus, so even our bodies become like his. When he is encountered face-to-face, even the physical body will become a perfect medium for the inner life and workings of the Holy Spirit. The body, the soul, and the spirit will be perfect and whole. The workings of the brain and all of the sensory organs will be perfect and complete. The body and mind will be free from the effects of sin and death. It is toward this goal that Jesus calls each of us Christians to move, day by day, until the final culmination of life when we see him face-to-face.

The Power of Jesus Now

The power that enables Jesus to transform these humiliated bodies of ours is, of course, no mere human power. Nothing human can match the power of the risen Christ. No matter what depths of relaxation we attain during prayer, on a strictly human level we can never come close to the depth of peace and power that Jesus himself communicates to us. Our source for physical rejuvenation needs to be more than human, for human measures will always result in eventual death. Through the Scriptures we are promised that our commonwealth is in heaven and eternal life is ours. In Luke 17:21, Jesus states that the kingdom is among us — now. Because of this, the power of Jesus can be felt in our bodies in the here and now — today. This power will be brought to complete and total fulfillment on the day of our entrance into the kingdom of heaven.

The power of Jesus allows him to subject all things to himself. *"Therefore God has highly exalted him and bestowed on him the name which is above every name, that at the name of Jesus every knee should bow, in heaven and on earth and under the earth, and every tongue confess that Jesus Christ is Lord, to the glory of God the Father.''* (Philippians 2:9-11) The Greeks to whom Paul was writing readily recognized this type of subjection; Paul used a military term that conveyed the idea of arranging persons or events under the authority of a ruler. The supreme authority of love and healing — our Lord Jesus — brings into subjection all the effects of sin and death caused by the fall of Adam that resulted in the humiliation of our bodies. Jesus subjects this sin and death to himself in order to free us from it. As we attune ourselves to him, especially through depth of prayer and meditation, we become open and receptive to the living power of Jesus Christ at work in our bodies.

The Body and the Holy Spirit

Jesus knew of this power which would cause transformation even in his own body. *''Destroy this temple, and in three days I will raise it up,''* he declared. The Jews then said, *''It has taken forty-six years to build this temple, and will you raise it up in three days?''* (John 2:19,21) Jesus foresaw the destruction of his physical body, the pain and eventual death he would have to endure. He also recognized that by the power within him any pain or destruction inflicted by the world would be transformed into resurrection life.

With assurance in his words, Jesus plainly said that his body would be raised up on the third day. Since Jesus was the forerunner of our faith, this must mean that we, too, will experience physical change and healing despite the occurrence of pain inflicted by living in the world. Our bodies will become entirely whole only when we enter into the ''new heaven and the new earth.'' (See Revelation 21:1-4.) But because the kingdom of heaven is already within us and among us, the resurrection power that can heal and make our bodies whole must be available to us even now.

As we live more in harmony with the spirit of Jesus, we can experience a gradual recuperation from bodily dysfunctions that may be stress-related. The American Academy of Family Physicians recently commented that over two-thirds of general office visits are precipitated by stress-related symptoms that indicate injury or destruction of some element or elements of bodily function. Harmful stress results from accumulated tensions of day-to-day living that are never released or resolved. Remedying those tensions through Christian meditation can result in a gradual recuperation of bodily function. In this sense, the resurrection life that was won for us by Jesus actually heals and transforms our physical cells. Jesus is a God of peace, not of stress. His peace, which surpasses all understanding, guards not only our inner spirits but also our bodies and gradually causes them to become like his own.

To the Greek mind, description of the body as a temple of the Holy Spirit had specific meaning. Two Greek words can be used for the single English word "temple." *Hieron* means a place that has been hallowed or consecrated. It refers to a building set apart for worship — any type of building, no matter what its former purpose, that has worship as its main function.

Hieron describes the whole compass of the sacred building. This includes porticos, courts, and any adjoining structures used for congregational worship. In New Testament Greek, the primary structure and all adjoining buildings are referred to as *hieron*.

The second Greek word for temple is *naos*, used to denote the Holy of Holies and the Holy Place. *Naos* does not describe the building set aside for worship. It refers to the inner holy place.

The *naos* is differentiated from *hieron* in that *naos* is the most sacred part of the temple. For example, *hieron* was used to designate the entire temple of Jerusalem during New Testament times. *Naos* referred solely to the Holy Place and Holy of Holies.

The veil of the temple that was rent in two at the death of our Lord Jesus was the veil of the *naos*. This veil separated the Holy of Holies from the Holy Place. The redeeming blood of Jesus penetrated into the very *naos* of the temple, the innermost place where the pure presence of God resided. The New Testament notes that when Zechariah entered the temple to worship, he entered the *naos*, the Holy Place. The people at large stood in the *hieron*. Only the chosen and select could enter the *naos* and experience the choicest blessings of God.

Saint Paul speaks of the body of the Christian as the *naos* of the Holy Spirit. The physical being of a man or a woman is likened to the inner sanctuary of the Holy Spirit. This can manifest the holiness and glory of God as truly as did the Holy of Holies in the temple at Jerusalem. Saint Paul does not think of the body as a mere external element of the Christian spiritual life. The body is the inner sanctuary, the most holy place, where the Holy Spirit resides.

Stress and the Holy Spirit

Just as the Holy Spirit can influence the physical body in a positive way, emotional stress and anxiety can influence it in a negative way. Psychologists have developed what is known as the Holmes-Rahe scale to measure the degree of emotional, psychological, and social stress experienced by an individual. Some of the highest stressors include divorce, the death of a spouse, marital separation, and the death of a close family member. Research in this area concludes that severe emotional and social stress can cause ulcers, psychological disturbances, broken bones, and other health problems as long as two years after the stress has been experienced.

The stresses of day-to-day living can weaken and deteriorate bodily functioning. For this very reason, Saint Paul encourages us to respect our bodies. Peaceful, harmonious attunement with the Holy Spirit counteracts the debilitating effects of stress. The work of the Holy Spirit invigorates and revitalizes the body as well as the spirit.

The fullness of the Holy Spirit influences and impacts the physical body in a way we can actually experience. When Jesus spoke of sending the Holy Spirit (John 14:16-17), he was referring to the Comforter. The Greek word for comfort meant "to call alongside." The Holy Spirit works alongside, comes to the aid of, our physical needs.

To the Greeks the word comforter designated "one called in to support or give aid to another." The Holy Spirit supports and aids the Christian in all dimensions of life. The Comforter contributes to the total salvation of the Christian: spirit, mind, and body.

In the Greek legal system the term for comforter also refers to a lawyer who provides aid to the accused. In this context the Holy

Spirit aids the believer to find comfort and solace from accusations of guilt and condemnation produced by a not-fully-redeemed conscience. Rather than allow the individual to sink into depths of despair, the Holy Spirit redeems guilt feelings by touches of grace and implants feelings of freedom within the soul.

Since we no longer operate under the law but under grace, a more appropriate translation of the comforter would be "one called in to help or provide consolation." As we grow more in the likeness of Jesus and become less attached to rigid legal systems, the realm of anointed consolation from the Holy Spirit opens up to us. Then, in times of emotional and spiritual need the Holy Spirit embraces the believer with blessings of peace and serenity. With this type of blessing we experience the Spirit as Comforter.

One evening, after I had given a teaching on the work of the Holy Spirit in the physical body, a woman approached me and shared her experience. For ten years she had suffered from intense migraine headaches whenever she would be in a large group of people. The headaches were apparently induced by the stress of having so many people around making demands on her. As she learned to utilize the Jesus Prayer and allow it to deeply relax her, she noted that even when she was in a very large group her migraines were no longer occurring. This woman knew the peace which surpasses all understanding, as the Comforter blessed her with such serenity that her physical reaction to stress subsided.

"Be Filled with the Spirit"

The Sacred Scriptures not only refer to the Holy Spirit as the Comforter but also call us to be filled with the presence of the Comforter. *"Be filled with the Spirit."* (Ephesians 5:18) The author of Ephesians calls the Christian forth to the inner life that drinks deeply of the presence of the Holy Spirit.

The imperative voice of this Scripture requires the believer to live a Christ-centered life. The Scripture firmly commands that the Holy Spirit be allowed to inspire what we say, what we do, and how we feel. A Christ-centered life encourages the believer to relinquish control of all aspects of personal life to the influence of the Holy Spirit. The imperative quality of this verse indicates the importance of yielding all facets of life to the infilling of the Holy Spirit.

The tense of the verb in "be filled" indicates the ongoing action of the infilling of the Holy Ghost. The work of the Holy Spirit within the heart of the believer is not a spasmodic filling up but a moment-by-moment penetration into the depths of the heart. As John the Baptizer declared, *"He must increase, but I must decrease."* (John 3:30) This inflow of the healing presence of God results from a moment-to-moment yielding to him. The Spirit longs to enter in and saturate as much of our being as we yield to him.

The implied plural subject of the scriptural bidding indicates that *all* men and women have the opportunity to encounter and soak in the presence of the living Christ. The Holy Spirit is not somehow especially delegated to a select few. Everyone who believes is called to be filled with the Spirit. Everyone who believes may enter into the Holy of Holies and know him who formed them and knew them in their mother's womb. All those who desire to drink deeply of the waters of life may do so.

Our society has begun to see the value of allowing time to get in touch with the refreshing presence of God within. Business and industry are recognizing the importance of allowing time for all individuals to settle themselves, to center themselves, and, for the Christian, to drink deeply of the Holy Spirit. Industrial firms on both Coasts now provide meditation breaks, because research shows that employees accomplish far more work if they are permitted to take a refreshing pause for meditation during the course of the day. Meditation and prayer do not belong only within the confines of the monastery or church.

The Holy Spirit, the Comforter, beckons to the heart of every man and woman to yield to him. As egocenteredness and selfishness are relinquished, the Holy Spirit radiates into the depths of the heart, going so deep as to cause even positive physical effects. The comforting action of the Holy Spirit resounds in the body. As believers yield themselves through peaceful prayer and meditation, muscles relax, blood pressure decreases, oxygen consumption decreases, and a general sense of physical well-being permeates the entire body.

Healed, Adopted, Glorified

The primary reason why the Holy Spirit influences our physical functioning in such a divine manner has to do with the fact that we have been *"bought with a price."* (1 Corinthians 6:20) The death of Jesus won our salvation. The shedding of his blood gives us access to the heavenly courts by cleansing us of sin. By his death and the cleansing power of his blood, we can enter into heavenly realms of experience. The price that the Father paid for your soul and mine was the blood of Jesus.

Before our redemption, Satan ruled the events of our lives and even our physical bodies. But the Father used the divine blood to purchase our souls from the ownership of Satan. The demonic powers at work in the world, in the lives of people, and in the physical body have been defeated by the blood of Jesus. Christ Jesus and the power of his Spirit now exert a gentle healing force within the human heart. Being cleansed by the blood of Jesus allows the believer to experience healing both spiritually and physically.

Jesus sacrificed his life so that we might have new life. The old life lived before conversion was the life of pain, burden, despair, and hopelessness. By the death of Jesus and the cleansing of his blood, the Christian now partakes of a deeper meaning in life. Life now involves union with the Father, the Son, and the Holy Spirit. Because Jesus bought us with the price of his life, we may now enjoy fruits of new life spiritually and physically.

Sons and Daughters of God

The Sacred Scriptures refer to Christians as adopted sons and daughters of God (Romans 9:26; Galatians 3:26; Ephesians 1:5; 2 Corinthians 6:18; 1 Thessalonians 5:5). We have been taken out of the realm of meaninglessness and despair, and adopted into the heavenly realm of meaningful living and richness of experience with the Father. We once belonged to the darkness of Satan. Now we have been adopted into God's family.

The English word *son* comes from the Greek word *huios*. The word for adoption is *huiothesia*. Literally, this compound word means "placing as a son." The Father placed us as his sons and daughters in his kingdom with no requirement on our part except that we receive the cleansing of the blood of Jesus. Thus, as adoptive sons and daughters of God, we were taken out of the realm of darkness and placed in the realm of Jesus.

The word *adoption* was used in New Testament times to refer to a Roman legal practice. It referred to a legal action in which a family would take in a child not its own. The family would do this for the purpose of giving the child all of the privileges and love accorded to a natural child. The adopted child would be legally entitled to all of the privileges and rights of a natural-born child. Romans 8:15 states clearly that we have received the spirit of sonship. The closeness and intimacy of the Father is conveyed through our position as his sons and daughters.

Romans 8:23 declares that our mortal bodies will not experience the fullness of what it means to be a son and daughter of God until the time when we meet him face-to-face. That is to say, even though believers have already been placed in the family of God, the physical body will not experience full glorification until the time of future glory in the New Jerusalem. As the future hope of total union with the Father is fulfilled, even our physical being will possess all the well-being and healing that spiritual adoption involves.

Glorifying God in Our Bodies

We have been bought with a price, and we are on this earth to glorify God in our bodies. A daily time of quiet and peace in the refreshing presence of our heavenly Father places us in contact with the glory that, someday, we will contain in totality. Because we have been bought with a price, we can now enter into at least partial contact with a glory so profound that even the physical body can be refreshed, soothed, and renewed. In the midst of day-to-day work and activity, we have the opportunity to be blessed spiritually, emotionally, and physically by the glory of the Father.

Because he has bought us with the price of the blood of his Son Jesus, we are to glorify our heavenly Father even in our bodies. The word *glory* refers to the countenance of the Father. Just as people display different types of countenances, so the Father manifests a countenance of glory. A person's countenance expresses inner feelings. For instance, people who feel very depressed often manifest a dark countenance, even to the extent that facial features may have tinges of gray. Such a depressed countenance betrays inner feelings of gloom and sadness. The Father's countenance reveals the glory that issues forth from his heart of love.

As the believer grows into the loving character expressed in the person of Jesus, so the glory of the Father will radiate from the inner soul outward to the body. The human frame discloses the glory of God felt within the inner soul. As our spiritual being is gradually transformed into the likeness of Jesus, our earthly frame undergoes the transformation that he underwent even while on this earth.

Mark 9:2 recalls the Transfiguration of Jesus on the Mount. As he encountered the glory of the Father, while speaking to Moses and Elijah, Jesus' earthly frame was transfigured. Even his clothes became whiter than any earthly bleach could make them. Because he was the pioneer on our journey to the Father, the glory Jesus experienced in his relationship to the Father is available to us. That is to say, the earthly body has the potential to be touched and transfigured in a manner similar to that experienced by Jesus on the Mount of Transfiguration.

Because the body is the temple of the Holy Spirit and because Christians are called to glorify God in their bodies, the importance of the body in the spiritual life is clear. The Father calls men and women not just as spiritual beings but as emotional and physical beings as well. The salvation won by Jesus through the shedding of his blood brings about a new birth spiritually and a potential healing and transformation physically. In order to become attuned to the glory of the Father, daily quiet times for prayer and meditation are of great value. As the body is attuned daily to the peaceful flow of the Holy Spirit within, rest and calm permeate the physical temple of the Holy Spirit. You are that temple — a temple of inner calm.

5
CALM CAN CHANGE YOUR LIFE

The temple of inner calm changes a person's life experience in at least three ways:

1. It develops a quiet confidence with regard to everyday living.
2. It fosters creativity that inspires personal achievement.
3. It cultivates compassion that increases our capacity to love ourselves and others in spite of faults and failings.

Confidence

Confidence literally means "with faith." To approach daily living with confidence means approaching it with faith. As Christians we understand that this faith is an inner assurance of God's providential caring for us and an assurance of our own God-given inner resources to accomplish the task at hand. Inner calm permits us to deal positively with life's responsibilities without anxiety and, thus, with confidence — a quiet confidence.

But my righteous one shall live by faith,
  and if he shrinks back,
  my soul has no pleasure in him.
But we are not of those who shrink back and are destroyed,
but of those who have faith and keep their souls.

(Hebrews 10:38-39)

We are called as Christians to live by a faith that moves us ahead to deal effectively with life's challenges. We are not to shrink back from difficulties or discouraging situations.

Shrinking back from the challenges of life destroys our sense of inner well-being. It is as if we as humans are meant to master life's difficulties and thereby acquire increasing self-confidence. This passage from Hebrews describes a process in which faith causes us to be able to keep our souls. To put this another way, using faith to deal with life's circumstances causes us to know who we are, to have a solid sense of self.

The Case of Hazel

This solid, confident sense of self is in direct opposition to the fearful anxiety that would cause us to shrink away from life. Quite frequently, clients with whom I have worked have described anxiety as causing them to feel like they are shrinking away. They feel extremely ineffective and inadequate, overwhelmed in the face of life's problems. A weakness, a heartfelt trembling, and intense interior tension grip them.

In contrast to this, a woman whom I will call Hazel described to me how inner calm fortified her with a quiet confidence of faith. For at least ten years Hazel had awakened each morning with a great deal of panic and dread. Her stomach would be contracting. A headache would usually be pounding away. Her heart would be palpitating.

This condition had occurred for so long that she could no longer even remember what had initially caused it. Morning after morning was filled with the dread of waking up to overwhelming fear. As the day progressed Hazel would actually tremble and shake at the thought of leaving her home. Going to the grocery store was a painful experience of encountering a hostile and insensitive world.

Nighttime allowed her some respite in knowing that the torturous feelings of the day were almost over.

No one seemed to understand the severity of Hazel's emotional and spiritual anguish. Her husband believed that she should just shape up and get out there and find a job. Her children began to refer to her as "old, neurotic Mom." She no longer had any friends since her old friends had grown weary of hearing the same old complaints.

One Saturday afternoon Hazel decided that she would force herself out of the house and attend a Legion of Mary meeting at her local parish. That afternoon I was speaking to the assembly on the practice of the Jesus Prayer. Hazel was very encouraged to learn of something that might help her in her daily battle with life. She talked to me after the presentation and assured me that she was going to implement it that very day. She also asked if she could call me if she had any questions. I assured her that I would be available to assist her in any way that I could.

I did not hear from Hazel again for at least three months. As it happened, the next time we saw each other was in the aisle of a local supermarket. I almost did not recognize her. She carried herself with a sense of surety and confidence. When I asked her how she was doing, she replied that she was continuing to use the Jesus Prayer daily and feeling very blessed by its effects.

Hazel told me that during the first week she felt almost nothing from the two twenty-minute periods of prayer a day. However, by the second week a distinct interior settledness began to fill her. As the days and the weeks went by, this interior settledness and calm grew. At times Hazel still had slight twinges of anxiety. But the decrease in her symptoms had been so evident that now her entire family seemed much happier. I definitely knew that she was feeling better when she spontaneously put down her grocery bag and gave me a big hug, thanking me for introducing her to the Jesus Prayer.

A Young Professor

Quite often it takes a bit longer than three months for the quiet confidence produced by the Jesus Prayer to take hold within a person. A young professor I once worked with had severe symptoms of inadequacy and inferiority. When I talked with him, he would not look me straight in the eye. He would mumble and talk so quietly I could hardly hear him. Throughout his life he had suffered from feelings of anxiety caused by an unconscious notion that he was inferior.

When he began using the Jesus Prayer, the young professor noticed an almost immediate relief from his muscle tension headaches, his trembling sensations whenever he walked into the classroom, and his anxiety in crowds. However, his lack of confidence with regard to dealing on a one-to-one basis with people continued for seven to eight months. During this time, psychotherapy assisted him in releasing and resolving his underlying feelings of inadequacy. We learned that during his early childhood his father and other significant males would belittle him whenever he attempted to express himself. They would refer to him as "a cocky little brat who was good for nothing."

Unfortunately, his first-grade teacher was also a male who used harshness and criticism to keep the children in line. Whenever he made mistakes in his schoolwork or in his behavior, the teacher would harshly reprimand him. Due to lack of adequate staff the school asked his first teacher to stay with the children through the second grade. Consequently, he was exposed for two elementary school years to a very harsh and critical male figure.

These combined experiences suffocated his confidence and self-worth. For many years he suffered the pain of believing that he was inadequate and inferior to most people. A lack of confidence permeated his childhood and early adult years.

The Jesus Prayer helped him in at least two ways. First of all, it produced the initial sense of ease and quietness within him so that his conflictual feelings of inferiority could more easily surface. Prior to this time he was so tense that he was not even able to talk about his feelings, much less release and resolve them. His daily meditation lowered his anxiety-ridden defenses enough to permit him to express and release his feelings within the therapeutic context.

The second help was that focusing on the name of Jesus reinforced and complimented our therapeutic gains. The young professor experienced an emotional catharsis and strengthening as a result of psychotherapy. Together with this, the Jesus Prayer filled him with the peace of God. As feelings of inferiority and inadequacy were released, God's own peace replaced them. As he grew in peace, he grew in self-confidence.

Contentment and Stability

"And without faith it is impossible to please him." (Hebrews 11:6) Without faith it is impossible to be content and pleased in our relationship with God, because we are in no way pleased with ourselves. Without exercising a faith-filled confidence, a daily discontent grips our souls. Feeling contentment, or taking pleasure in our own well-being, cannot take place without the bedrock of confidence.

For the soul, quiet confidence is like a firmly planted anchor. When trials and vexations come, quiet confidence offers stability and security. Human souls seem to lean easily toward emotional shattering and discontent. The storms of life can easily cause a severe battering and uprooting. For this reason the quiet confidence produced by the Jesus Prayer offers an antidote to potential emotional shattering and chaos.

During my first clinical psychopathology course in graduate school, I remember a professor noting that a lack of personal confidence and significant anxiety were hallmarks of emotional chaos. Troubled souls question their self-worth. They experience the world as hostile and frightening. They frequently view other people as antagonistic and hostile. Lack of confidence and intense anxiety usually precipitate this sort of emotional fragility.

Freud and other analysts have commented on the role of anxiety and calmness in emotional well-being as if they had discovered something new. Long before Freud, Jesus explicitly referred to calmness and peace. Before leaving his disciples, he assured them, *"Peace I leave with you, my peace I give to you."* Jesus knew that only with calmness and peace would the apostles and disciples have the confidence necessary to meet the demands of a growing Church. His peace reinforces within us a confidence to meet all the demands of life.

111

You may wonder why I am emphasizing the importance of confidence in daily living. Even after all I have stated to this point, it may seem like an arduous task to pray daily in order to acquire deeply felt confidence. Such an undertaking may seem too great or too burdensome for you.

I am aware that confidence will positively influence your daily living in at least three ways: It contributes to a personal sense of well-being; it instills greater motivation and potential to follow through with responsibilities of life; it provides the greater energy to accomplish what God has planned for you in life.

A Sense of Well-being

A personal sense of well-being is developed during meditation because there you lovingly encounter the very God who created you. God's own sense of wholeness and well-being is communicated to you. He created you in his own image and likeness. His image and likeness exudes with wholeness and well-being. Your innermost self becomes saturated with God's own sense of well-being as you spend daily time with him.

A young man shared with me how the Jesus Prayer nourished his personal sense of well-being. In other types of prayer he would frequently become very tense in trying to concentrate on the presence of God. He would think of what he wanted to say to God. His mind seemed to be more occupied on what to say to God than it was occupied on God's presence. Prayer for him was a chore.

In his words, "With the Jesus Prayer I am receptive in the presence of God. I do not have to work to attain an awareness of his presence. I am in him and he is in me. As I say his name I feel good and full inside."

Motivation for Responsibility

Along with a personal sense of well-being the Jesus Prayer can assist you to have the motivation to follow through with the responsibilities of life. Anxiety and worry consume a great deal of energy. If energy is consumed in such a manner, you may frequently feel depleted and drained. Daily time spent in prayerful meditation gradually dissolves such anxiety and worry.

As energy is no longer funneled into anxiety and worry, it can be used to meet the responsibilities of life. Usually, you will experience this as a renewed motivation to follow through with the tasks that are set before you. You will feel alive and invigorated to meet the challenges of life.

A middle-aged man candidly admitted that for a period of thirty days he had stayed home, literally pulled the bed covers over his head, and worried. He was a salesman who had experienced a series of rejections in his day-to-day work. Worry and anxiety got such a hold on him that he was terrified to approach life. He stayed at home hoping that his problems would vanish.

As he began the process of meditation his anxieties and worries would come to mind. He told me, ''When I thought of all these things I would do just what you said. I would let them float out of my mind like a cloud through the sky and return to focusing on the name of Jesus. Little by little my mind was focused more on Jesus than on my worry. Over a few weeks time I felt that I had the confidence and energy to return to work. My mind was more focused on God than on my problems now.''

The practice of the Jesus Prayer provided this salesman with renewed energy to succeed and accomplish his business goals. He remarked to me that after seven hours of sleep he would feel refreshed. He could hardly wait to get out the door and meet his new prospects.

Before coming home from work he would spend twenty minutes in his office meditating on the name of Jesus. When he arrived home his spirit was at peace. His family began to look forward to their time in the evening with him. His refreshment and confidence passed on renewed vitality to them.

Within twelve months he set the state record for sales in his field. He was honored by being given a small plaque for outstanding achievement. He remarked, ''That plaque not only helped me to remember my business achievements, it helped me to remember my spiritual and emotional achievements.''

The energy this man achieved is one of the by-products of a consistent prayer life. As the soul is quieted, its natural energies come forth. Once personal energy is unlocked from anxieties it seems to naturally be propelled toward accomplishments.

The Prophet Elijah

The prophet Elijah in the Old Testament is an example of a man of God who grew in confidence and accomplishments as the result of overcoming his anxieties. He is considered the prophet of fire. In appearance he resembled John the Baptizer. His features were rugged, his clothing unkempt, and his mannerisms crude. God called Elijah to be his mighty prophet. Yet, Elijah knew discouragements and anxieties.

In his early life Elijah told Ahab, the king of Israel, that Israel would receive no rain for a number of years because of the king's sinfulness. After this prophecy the Lord commanded Elijah to go out into the wilderness in the Kerith Ravine. There the Lord miraculously provided for Elijah's every need. In the desert Elijah drank from a brook of fresh springwater. Ravens brought him bread and meat in the morning and evening.

Later, the Lord sent Elijah to a widow in Zarephath to be fed. On his arrival the prophet asked the woman for a drink of water and a piece of bread. She told him that her supply had been reduced to a handful of flour and a little oil in a jug. Elijah assured her that as she provided for him so the Lord would provide for her. The widow made a small cake of bread for Elijah, providing for his needs in accordance with what God asked. Throughout the drought the flour in her jar and the oil in the jug never lessened despite daily usage. Elijah even raised the widow's son from the dead, a blessing to her as a result of her faithfulness to God.

Perhaps the most dramatic of events in Elijah's life took place on Mount Carmel. The 450 prophets of Baal and the 400 prophets of Asherah were summoned by Elijah to the Mount. In order to prove the power of Yahweh and the vanity of false gods, Elijah challenged the false prophets. He told them to place a bull on the altar of their god. The prophets were not to light the bull on fire as a sacrifice. Instead, they were to ask their god to consume the bull by sending fire from heaven. From morning until midday the prophets prayed and wailed for their god to answer them. A little past midday Elijah intervened.

He placed his bull on the altar to Yahweh. He even doused the bull with four large jars of water. The water ran down the altar and filled the trench surrounding the altar. When Elijah prayed, the fire of the Lord fell from the heavens and consumed the bull. Once again God had worked miraculously and powerfully through Elijah.

After his victory on Carmel, Elijah was faced with another problem. King Ahab told the wicked Queen Jezebel how all of the prophets had been defeated and killed. Jezebel threatened Elijah's life. With great trepidation and anxiety Elijah fled from Jezebel.

After a day's journey in the desert he stopped under a juniper tree. Filled with desperation, Elijah prayed that God would take his life. Under the weight of such stress and burden he fell asleep.

The Scriptures record that an angel of the Lord then came to Elijah. The angel provided a cake of bread baked over hot coals and a jar of water. The angelic messenger encouraged Elijah to continue his journey. Strengthened by the food and drink, Elijah traveled forty days and forty nights to Mount Horeb.

At Mount Horeb the Lord appeared to Elijah. Anticipating God's word coming to him, Elijah waited quietly in a cave on the Mount. First a very powerful wind came. The wind tore the mountains apart and shattered the rocks. God's presence, however, was not in this manifestation. Next an earthquake came. But the presence of God was not in the earthquake. After the earthquake came a fire. The word of God was not in the fire. Finally, in a very gentle whisper the word of God came to Elijah and inspired him to carry out his mission.

In times of intense anxiety Elijah's confidence was restored by retreating into calm and quiet. Only after he fell asleep in the desert did the angel minister to him. Through the tranquillity of sleep Elijah's receptivity to God was restored. At this point, and only at this point, could the angel minister to him.

In the cave on Mount Horeb, Elijah expected a flashy manifestation of God to inspire and encourage him. But the depth of God's presence was not communicated in a flashy manner. Neither the powerful wind nor the earthquake nor the fire brought the word of God. God's word was carried most powerfully in gentleness and quietness. Calmness most purely conveyed God's word to Elijah. A divinely ordained calmness generated the confidence Elijah required in order to carry out his responsibilities.

In gentleness, quietness, and calmness lies our confidence. Great confidence to handle day-to-day living will be communicated to you as you set aside time daily to spend in your personal cave within. Divine confidence will be generated within you as you hear God's gentle whispers, assuring you of his love for you. The calmness cultivated by the Jesus Prayer allows divine confidence to saturate us. The confidence transmitted to Elijah on top of Mount Horeb will be freely given to you as you spend time alone with him in quietness and calmness.

Creativity

Along with the transmission of confidence, calmness accentuates creative potential. Creativity is the inspiration that underlies all new ideas, discoveries, and inventions.

The story is told of the chemist Kekule struggling with the formation of a specific chemical molecule. Day and night he pondered over the structure of this molecule. Relentlessly, he wondered about how this molecule could be formed.

One afternoon Kekule wearily fell asleep. During this sleep he dreamed of the structure of this molecule. The image in the dream was that of a snake curved into a circle. When he saw this image in his dream, he recognized this as being the formation of the chemical molecule he had been seeking.

During times of intense work and concentration our intellectual faculties often require rest and tranquillity before creativity surfaces. This creativity comes in the form of discoveries, artistic work, and the formulation of new ideas. Intense concentration provides, as it were, the fuel for the fire. But the fire is not lit until we are in a receptive and calm mood. Calmness generates profound creativity.

In the Acts of the Apostles it is reported that Saint Peter was confronted by an extremely challenging problem that called for divine inspiration and creativity. A Gentile named Cornelius desired that the word of God be made known to him. When confronted with this opportunity, Peter felt repulsed at the thought of entering a Gentile home with the sacred word of God.

Chapter 10 of Acts records that Peter went up on the roof of his home to pray. In the quietness of prayer he had a vision of the heavens opening up and a large sheet being let down to earth by its four corners. On this sheet were all kinds of four-footed animals, reptiles, and birds. A voice commanded Peter, *"Rise, Peter; kill and eat."* But Peter refused to eat such unclean creatures. The voice assured him, *"What God has cleansed, you must not call common."*

The inspiration that Peter experienced during prayer provided a solution to his problem. Prior to this it would have been unthinkable for a Jewish man to enter a Gentile house for the purpose of spreading God's word. Peter's prayer life opened him up to God creating a new way. What was considered impossible became possible through divine creativity. During the quietness of prayer, Peter was inspired with creativity that literally changed the world.

A chronic state of anxiety would not have permitted Peter to have received God's creative word. Anxiety and tension interfere with the process of creativity. The waters of creativity can be dammed up by walls of anxiety.

Anxiety Inhibits Creativity

Anxiety produces a high intensity and frequency of brain waves. Thus, mental capabilities are concentrated upon anxiety-ridden situations. The brain generates very intense, frantic waves in response to high levels of stress. In this sort of state, creativity is blocked. Anxiety, rather than relaxation and creativity, generates the electrical stimulation in the brain.

Creativity originates in the brain. Under conditions of intense and chronic anxiety, creativity is inhibited. Brain impulses reflect either a relaxed mood conducive to creativity or electrical waves reflective of anxiety. The two are mutually exclusive; the brain harbors either anxiety or creativity, but not both.

Just as the brain responds to anxiety, muscles in the body also mirror anxiety. Body muscles constrict, often to the point of pain, when the individual is under chronic tension. Muscles in the forehead, the neck, the lower back, and the stomach are the most frequent respondents to high levels of anxiety.

Such muscle constriction interferes with the body's capacity to engage in creative performance. Athletes are known to "choke" from experiencing performance anxiety. Under such conditions athletic performance is cramped.

In a recent behavioral medicine seminar that I attended, the example was given of a professional skier "choking." Before leaving the gate for the ski jump the skier's back and leg muscles would cramp. Obviously, this incapacitated him. It was determined that the cramping was the result of severe performance anxiety. Once the anxiety was dealt with, the skier went on to set a new regional record. Anxiety inhibited his creative performance. Calmness released his creative performance.

I have also noticed that academic performance can be drastically affected by the measure of anxiety or calmness in a person's life. Peter, a young man I was treating, flunked out of school prior to beginning therapy with me. He could not seem to concentrate on his subjects. Teachers had commented that he seemed to have a high intellectual capacity that was never manifested in his work.

During our first session Peter had symptoms of intense agitation, jitteriness, restlessness, and a high level of distractability. He remarked that many of these symptoms began when he and his family had suffered a severe falling-out two years before. He had rebelled against many of the values and behaviors that were expected of him by his parents. The family could not constructively resolve these conflicts. Consequently, Peter continued to rebel.

Throughout this time his school grades worsened. He had a history of making grades of A's and B's. With the onslaught of this family conflict his grades plummeted to F's. He blamed a great deal of this on his own level of internal anxiety.

After four months of psychotherapy, a great deal of Peter's rebellion and anxiety had been worked through. He began using the Jesus Prayer on a daily basis at this time. He noted an immediate sense of bodily relaxation and mental ease. He felt that he wanted to return to school.

During his first semester at a local university Peter managed to attain a 3.0 grade average. His subjects included areas in both the hard sciences and the liberal arts. Needless to say, he was extremely pleased at his performance.

Utilization of the Jesus Prayer promotes such an internalization of peace and calm that powers of concentration are sharpened. This creates the mental climate for creative performance and accomplishment. Such creativity can be in areas as diverse as school, sports, and science.

Compassion

The building of confidence and creativity would be for naught were they not to lead to the development of compassion. The Christian call is a call toward love. In the end, the development of love made manifest through compassion is the purpose of following Jesus.

Three primary forces potentially inhibit the flow of compassion. These forces are anger, guilt, and fear. The calm and peace induced by the Jesus Prayer act as healing agents in each of these areas. Anger, guilt, and fear can be transformed into a depth of Christian compassion.

The Letter to the Ephesians exhorts Christians to *"Be angry but do not sin."* (Ephesians 4:26) In other words, anger in and of itself is not wrong. Anger is an emotion that can be expressed appropriately and, therefore, not sinfully.

When anger is directed briefly and succinctly to the situation at hand, rather than toward injuring or hurting another person, it can be appropriate. Anger of this sort seeks expression in order to obtain a constructive resolution of the problem. It seeks the betterment of all individuals involved.

Sinful anger is anger that is long held to the point of bitterness. It seeks to promote emotional injury and hurt. Sinful anger aims at belittling, criticizing, and destroying the good.

Oftentimes we can attempt to rationalize sinful anger under the pretense that *we deserve to be angry because we are right*. Out of the sense of "being right" anger is harbored within. It becomes bitterness and, eventually, rage.

The Case of the Angry Elder

Once, after I gave a presentation on anger to a local Protestant church group, one of the elders walked up to me and said, "But you don't understand, Doctor DeBlassie. I really do deserve to be angry. In this situation I am right. One year ago my pastor told me I could prepare to give a Scripture study on the Gospel of John to the church. I prepared for that Scripture study for six months. One month ago he told me that I would no longer be able to give the Scripture study when I had intended. There was a conflict in the church schedule. I would have to wait. Doesn't he realize how long I prepared? I felt like he just pushed me to the side. I deserve to be angry."

As he told me all of this his face was flushed. The veins in his neck were protruding. He was practically out of breath. I didn't say a word; it was obvious that he was convinced that he deserved to be angry because "he was right."

Three months later I received a call from the man's wife. She asked if I had some time to visit him. He was in the cardiovascular care unit at the local hospital. Evidently, after another heated exchange with his pastor, he had suffered a heart attack. When I walked into the hospital room he looked at me and said, "I guess I know what you mean now."

As I sat and talked to him, he could hardly believe the damage his anger had caused him personally. He knew that the intensity of this long-held emotion had actually precipitated his heart attack. Fortunately, the knowledge of how destructive long-held anger could be helped to inspire him to change his way of dealing with anger.

I introduced him to the Jesus Prayer, and he began to practice it faithfully. Whenever he felt the temptation to bitterness, the practice of the Jesus Prayer would alleviate his inclination. In his words, "It is as if the calmness and peace that I feel during the Jesus Prayer just do not mix with anger. Either I stop praying or I stop being angry. They cannot both exist at the same time. I have decided to always continue my prayer life. I feel much more at peace now.''

Guilt and the Jesus Prayer

The feeling of guilt often is quick to follow anger. Guilt can be defined as that personal sense of remorse felt after wrongdoing. Guilt can be more debilitating than bitterness.

It is a well-known psychological phenomenon that guilt triggers unconscious self-punishment. I have witnessed individuals suffer from physical ailments, marital disharmony, and employment problems after having committed acts of wrongdoing. It is as if situations in a guilt-ridden person's life turn sour in order to punish the transgressor. Usually, the person is not even aware that guilt is the motivating force behind punishing life events. Unresolved remorse of this type debilitates both personal and interpersonal functioning.

A young minister with whom I worked suffered from intense guilt. In a weak moment he had become involved sexually with a prominent woman in the church. This was a one-day affair. He never came close to her again after committing this transgression.

Unfortunately, this woman became pregnant as a result of their sexual entanglement. Without consulting him, she immediately obtained an abortion. It so happened that he was away on vacation at the time. A day or two after her abortion she met with the church board to tell them about this tragedy. When the pastor came back to town, needless to say he was in shock. He had already been suffering from intense guilt as a result of having fallen into sexual sin. This woman's indiscretions further overwhelmed him with remorse and shame. He literally fled from the church and withdrew into his home. He withdrew from all contact with others.

An elderly woman in his congregation had engaged in inter-cessory prayer for him since he had come to the church. During his time of trial she would go to his home every day at noon. She would ring the doorbell and knock on the door.

After two weeks of this, he finally answered when the woman knocked. The moment he opened the door she embraced him. This elderly woman sat him down and told him that no matter what he ever did in his life, God still loved him. She assured him that she had been interceding for him since his arrival at the church.

Before he came to see me, this minister had been introduced to the Jesus Prayer by the elderly woman. Very firmly and gently she had guided him in its usage and application. She made it so simple and clear that he could not resist using it in his everyday life.

In his words, "During my time of turmoil I literally had no energy to pray. Getting out of bed in the morning required Herculian strength from me. In no way did I have the vitality and gumption to approach the presence of God in prayer. In using the Jesus Prayer, I was able to be at peace before God. It did not require strain and arduous effort to approach him. I merely relaxed and allowed myself to be aware of his presence. Focusing on the name of Jesus over and over helped to instill his presence within me. I did not have to reach out to him. In using the Jesus Prayer he came to me."

In later describing his experiences in prayer he likened them to being cuddled on the lap of the Father. In the midst of guilty feelings he felt God's love for him more and more. Soon, guilt gave way under the constant flow of God's love. In calmness and receptivity the Father's love saturated him. The Father's embracing love healed him from the clutching grip of guilt.

Once he was out from under the oppression of guilt, he was able to return to a very active and productive ministry. He moved to a different part of the country to begin afresh. The last time I saw him he remarked to me, "Being healed of my own sin and guilt helped me to feel much more compassion for others. I now feel that I can better reach out to heal the hurts in others since I now know what it's like to hurt deeply."

The Letter to the Hebrews states, *"let us draw near with a true heart . . . with our hearts sprinkled clean from an evil conscience."* (Hebrews 10:22) This word confirms that a cleansing of heart occurs in drawing near to God. Approaching the presence of God purifies the human heart from guilty transgression.

The Jesus Prayer allows us to approach the presence of God smoothly and deliberately. Without stress and strain we are able to enter into the loving embrace of the Father that heals all guilt.

Freedom from the bondage of guilt generates a new power to love with the healing compassion of Jesus.

Fear and the Jesus Prayer

Fear is an even deeper human emotion than guilt. Depth psychologists identify fear, not hate, as the opposite of love.

"Perfect love casts out fear." (1 John 4:18) Love vanquishes fear. A deficit of love increases fear. As love is present within human relationships, fear and all of its symptoms subside.

After a late night meeting I was once approached by a middle-aged woman who complained of her husband exhibiting the very symptoms of fear that I had described to the group that night. The husband constantly complained about shortness of breath, heart palpitations, feelings of apprehension, and an inability to concentrate. Also, he would spontaneously become very moody and withdrawn.

His wife dejectedly told me that he had been suffering from these symptoms for the entire fifteen years of their marriage. He refused to seek help because he felt he should be able to solve his own problems. As the years passed his symptoms of fear worsened. Out of desperation his wife sought my advice and assistance.

When I first saw the couple together in my office the man was very forlorn and withdrawn. His emotional expression was flat, and he seemed distant and reserved. He could hardly maintain eye contact with me.

I realized that this was all a manifestation of a deep underlying fear. As we sensitively explored his feelings, as far as he was able, it became evident that he had been raised in a family that propagated emotional neglect and distance. In essence, he never knew love, so he could never give love.

In therapy, the man admitted that feelings of personal isolation and alienation were overwhelming him. He literally felt unloved and unlovable. He approached other people, even members of his own family, with a great deal of fear and trembling. He was always afraid of saying something or doing something wrong. He was afraid of being criticized for one thing or another.

His fear was so intense that progress in psychotherapy proved very difficult. He would clam up and refuse to share his feelings and thoughts. This emotional constriction interfered with therapeutic progress.

Rather than continue in such a halting and stumbling way, we decided to experiment with the Jesus Prayer. I am referring to this as an experiment because I do not usually introduce the Jesus Prayer until the end, or near the end, of psychotherapy. The reason for this lies in the fact that the profound relaxation produced by the Jesus Prayer can often cause intense and unresolved areas of emotional conflict to surface quite spontaneously. This can prove to be very frightening, even terrifying. I have found it best to reach a point of release and resolution regarding major emotional conflicts before entering into the practice of the Jesus Prayer. But in this case, I proposed that we experience the Jesus Prayer at the beginning of therapy in order to see if somehow it might assist us in our therapeutic work.

Upon learning the process of the Jesus Prayer, the man diligently practiced it. In fact, he was one of the most disciplined meditators I had ever worked with. He conscientiously practiced the Jesus Prayer twice a day.

After one month he commented on feeling much more relaxed and at ease. His wife noted that he no longer tossed and turned in bed at night. Also a great deal of his moodiness subsided.

Within the context of therapy we all witnessed his increased ability to communicate his feelings. He could talk spontaneously and forthrightly about emotions of anger, depression, and fear. Unconscious emotional conflicts unraveled themselves from within him. He confirmed, ''The more I open up now, the easier it is for me to open up.''

Therapy lasted approximately six months. The Jesus Prayer, in this case, assisted us in finding emotional release. It primed the pump, so to speak. The practice of daily meditation relaxed him physically and emotionally, permitting the eventual release and resolution of painful feelings. Needless to say, the symptoms of fearfulness gradually dissolved. A combination of psychotherapy and regular practice of the Jesus Prayer caused a real depth of healing from fear.

Fear is perhaps the most devastating of all human emotions. But contact with the presence of the loving Jesus heals the deepest of fears. His perfect love heals all fear.

With the Jesus Prayer you allow yourself to be embraced by his perfect love for you. Whatever frightens you, whatever causes you guilt, whatever angers you is touched by his loving presence. No fear, no guilt, no anger can be maintained once you have felt his gentle touch of love.

He is calling you, *"Come unto me, all who labor and are heavy laden, and I will give you rest."* (Matthew 11:28)

Bibliography

Bible. Revised Standard Version.

Blois, Louis de. "Joined to God in the Divine Light." In *The Soul Afire*. Edited by H. A. Reinhold. Garden City, New York: Doubleday and Company, Inc., 1973.

Eckhart, Meister. "Answer to a Timid Worker." In *The Soul Afire*. Edited by H. A. Reinhold. Garden City, New York: Doubleday and Company, Inc., 1973.

Freud, Sigmund. *The Standard Edition of the Complete Psychological Works of Sigmund Freud*. Vol. 1, *Pre-psychoanalytic Publications and Unpublished Drafts*. London: Hogarth Press, 1966.

Guntrip, Harry. *Schizoid Phenomena, Object-relations, and the Self*. New York: International Universities Press, Inc., 1969.

Jung, C. G. *Psychology and Religion*. New Haven, Conn.: Yale University Press, 1938.

Marshall, Daniel P., J. Gregory Rabold, and Edgar S. Wilson. *Staying Healthy Without Medicine*. Chicago, Ill.: Nelson-Hall, 1983.

May, Rollo. *The Meaning of Anxiety*. Rev. ed. New York: W. W. Norton and Company, Inc., 1977.

Merton, Thomas. *The Wisdom of the Desert*. New York: Directions Publishing Corp., 1970.

Osuna, Francisco de. *The Third Spiritual Alphabet*. New York: Paulist Press, 1981.

Redfearn, J. W. T. "The Energy of Warring and Combining Opposites: Problems for the Psychotic Patient and the Therapist in Achieving the Symbolic Situation." In *Methods of Treatment in Analytical Psychology*. Edited by Ian F. Baker. Irving, Texas: Spring Publications, 1980.

Rolle, Richard. "O Sweet and Delectable Light." In *The Soul Afire*. Edited by H. A. Reinhold. Garden City, New York: Doubleday and Company, Inc., 1973.

Teresa of Avila, Saint. *The Book of Her Life*. In *The Collected Works of St. Teresa of Avila*. Trans. by O. Rodriguez and K. Kavanaugh. 2 vols. Washington, D.C.: Institute of Carmelite Studies, 1980.

————. *The Interior Castle*. In *The Collected Works of St. Teresa of Avila*. Trans. by O. Rodriguez and K. Kavanaugh. 2 vols. Washington, D.C.: Institute of Carmelite Studies, 1980.

————. *The Way of Perfection*. In *The Collected Works of St. Teresa of Avila*. Trans. by O. Rodriguez and K. Kavanaugh. 2 vols. Washington, D.C.: Institute of Carmelite Studies, 1980.

Thomas Aquinas, Saint. "God Intimately in Us." In *The Soul Afire*. Edited by H. A. Reinhold. Garden City, New York: Doubleday and Company, Inc., 1973.

Thomas á Kempis. *The Imitation of Christ*. Edited by Harold C. Gardiner. Garden City, New York: Doubleday and Company, Inc., 1955.

Winnicott, D. W. *The Maturational Processes and the Facilitating Environment*. New York: International Universities Press, Inc., 1965.

MORE MATERIAL ON PRAYER FROM LIGUORI

CONTEMPLATIVE PRAYER
A Guide for Today's Catholic
by James Borst, M.H.M.
A good, popular discussion of the what, why, and how of contemplative prayer for the ordinary person. **$1.95**

IN MY HEART ROOM
Sixteen Love Prayers for Little Children
by Mary Terese Donze, A.S.C.
A simple, easy-to-follow method to teach children a special way to pray. The book is to be used by the parent or teacher. **$1.95**

PRAYER: A Handbook for Today's Catholic
by Reverend Eamon Tobin
This handbook combines the theory and the experience of prayer to provide Catholics with a comprehensive and practical guide to improving their prayer lives. In one volume, this book considers four simple keys to successful prayer and presents more than a dozen different prayer styles along with information, techniques, and practical suggestions. **$4.95**

PRAYERS FOR MARRIED COUPLES
by Renee Bartkowski
This book contains over seventy-five brief prayers that express the hopes, the concerns, and the dreams of today's married couples. By using this book to pray aloud, couples can add a new and deeper dimension to their marriage. Shared prayer can lead them into a stronger union with God and into a more intimate relationship with each other. **$3.95**

THE HEALING POWER OF PRAYER
by Bridget Meehan, SCC, D.Min.
This powerful book helps readers find comfort and healing through prayer as they attempt to deal with pain, guilt, anxiety, loneliness, and depression. It considers the potential of healing from the Church's perspective and then introduces six types of healing prayer experiences. **$2.95**

Order from your local bookstore or write to:
Liguori Publications, Box 060, Liguori, MO 63057-9999
*(Please add $1.00 for postage and handling for orders
under $5.00; $1.50 for orders over $5.00.)*